Grammar Practice Workbook

GRADE 2

Requests for permission to make copies of any part of the work should be submitted through our Permissions website at https://customercare.hmhco.com/contactus/Permissions.html or mailed to Houghton Mifflin Harcourt Publishing Company, Attn: Rights Compliance and Analysis, 9400 Southpark Center Loop, Orlando, Florida 32819-8647.

Printed in the U.S.A.

ISBN 978-0-358-22680-2

1 2 3 4 5 6 7 8 9 10   0928   28 27 26 25 24 23 22 21 20 19

4500768328   A B C D E F G

Grade 2

Contents

Subjects

A **sentence** tells a complete thought. It has a naming part and an action part.

The **subject** is the naming part of a sentence. The subject tells who or what does or did something. The subject tells what the sentence is about.

Children play fun games.

▶ **Draw a line under the naming part of the sentence.**

1. Tomi ducks behind a door.

2. Kellie's dog barks.

3. Benny hides under the covers.

4. The boots leave muddy tracks.

▶ **Write the naming part from the box to finish the sentence.**

> **The cat**   **My uncle**

5. _____ tells funny stories.

6. _____ purrs in its bed.

▶ **Revisit a piece of your writing. Edit the draft to make sure subjects are used correctly.**

Predicates

A **predicate** is the action part of a sentence.

A predicate tells what the subject in a sentence does or did. The action part of a sentence uses words that show action.

Daniel **runs fast**.

▶ **Circle the word or words that tells the action in each sentence.**

1. Lukas reads a book.

   reads a book   a book

2. The team goes into the store.

   store   goes into the store

3. The friends ran down the street.

   the street   ran down the street

4. The teacher clapped her hands.

   clapped her hands   her hands

5. Jarred eats a sandwich.

   a sandwich   eats a sandwich

▶ **Revisit a piece of your writing. Edit the draft to make sure all predicates are used correctly.**

Using Sentences

▶ **Write the subject to finish each sentence.**

1. _____ sings a song. (Matt, If)

2. _____ writes a note. (Sophie, To)

3. _____ ask for a book. (Hear, The children)

4. _____ eats her dinner. (Ahmed, Now)

5. _____ liked the story. (Everyone, Throw)

▶ **Write the predicate to finish each sentence.**

6. Max _____. (ball, kicked a ball)

7. The scooter _____. (glides, then)

8. Everyone _____. (blew up balloons, the balloons)

9. Kameko _____. (a bat, swings a bat)

10. Some friends _____. (played jump rope, the rope)

▶ **Revisit a piece of your writing. Edit the draft to make sure all sentences are used correctly.**

Review Subjects and Predicates

▶ **Underline the subject in each sentence.**

1. Zoey ate the apple.

2. My mother hugs the dog.

3. Maci ate peanuts.

4. Frances went to the park.

5. My friend was happy to see me.

▶ **Circle the predicate in each sentence.**

6. Jiro fed his parrot.

7. Ashka ran down the path.

8. The brothers fished in the pond.

9. We shopped for new mittens.

10. Caleb blew his horn.

▶ **Revisit a piece of your writing. Edit the draft to make sure all subjects and predicates are used correctly.**

Connect to Writing: Using Subjects and Predicates Correctly

▶ **Read the selection and choose the best answer to each question.**

> *Riku wrote the following paragraph about playing at his friend's house. Read his paragraph and look for any revisions he should make. Then answer the questions that follow.*

(1) I went to Jerome's house. (2) Jerome played on the swings. (3) I threw the ball. (4) Jerome built a sand castle in the sandbox. (5) I built a sand castle in the sandbox. (6) Jerome into the treehouse. (7) We played hide-and-seek. (8) I think I will go to Jerome's tomorrow!

1. Which two sentences have the same predicate?

A. Sentences 1 and 2

B. Sentences 4 and 5

C. Sentences 1 and 8

D. Sentences 7 and 8

2. How can you improve sentence 6 by using a predicate?

A. Jerome climbed into the treehouse.

B. Jerome water into the treehouse.

C. Jerome hold into the treehouse.

D. Jerome cat into the treehouse.

▶ **What do you like to do with your friend? Write two or three sentences about it.**

Complete Sentences

A sentence tells what someone or something does or did.
A complete **simple sentence** has a **subject** (naming part) and a **predicate** (action part).

My mother bakes a cake.
Subject: My mother   **Predicate:** bakes a cake

▶ **Underline each complete simple sentence.**

1. Moves the brick.   Jon moves the brick.

2. And makes bread.   My grandma makes bread.

3. My shy cat.   My shy cat runs under the bed.

4. Martin eats his lunch.   His lunch.

5. Sunil closes the door.   Closes the door.

▶ **Circle the sentence part that is missing.**

6. Jack and Ashley _____.

   subject   predicate

7. _____ claps his hands.

   subject   predicate

▶ **Revisit a piece of your writing. Edit the draft to make sure all simple sentences are used correctly.**

Word Order in Sentences

When a sentence tells something, the subject comes first.
The predicate of a sentence comes next.

Incorrect Word Order	Correct Word Order
Ran fast we.	We ran fast.

▶ **Underline each sentence that has correct word order.**

1. The dog eats snacks.

2. Jerome pushed the cart.

3. Laughs out loud Harry.

4. The lunch was yummy.

5. All jump together we.

6. My sister ran up the stairs.

7. So much fun he had with them.

8. Children picked up the sticks.

9. Amal sees the airplane.

10. Paying the bill was Mom.

▶ **Revisit a piece of your writing. Edit the draft to make sure sentences have the correct word order.**

Run-On Sentences

> A **run-on sentence** is when two sentences run together without using punctuation.

▶ **If the sentence is a run-on sentence, circle YES. If the sentence is not a run-on sentence, circle NO.**

1. My brother played baseball. They went running.   YES   NO

2. We play in the park we find rocks.   YES   NO

3. Vicky and I sing together we are best friends.   YES   NO

4. My father works long hours. He is a dentist.   YES   NO

5. Janice kicks a ball she needs to practice.   YES   NO

6. My cousin likes to swim. She is at the pool.   YES   NO

7. Thomas eats lunch he has a sandwich.   YES   NO

8. Maria writes a letter she uses pink paper.   YES   NO

▶ **Rewrite each run-on sentence as two complete simple sentences.**

9. My sister learned to sing she took voice lessons.

_____

10. Luis got a pizza he shared it with us.

_____

▶ **Revisit a piece of your writing. Edit the draft to make sure there are no run-on sentences.**

Review Simple Sentences

A complete **simple sentence** has both a subject and a predicate. The **subject** tells who or what. The **predicate** tells what the subject did or does.

Subject	Predicate
Thomas	jumped.
My best friend	plays the piano.

▶ **Underline the group of words if it is a complete sentence.**

1. Wolves howl at night.

2. Shari's birthday.

3. Watched two shows!

4. The play was exciting.

5. Kyrie popped balloons.

6. Was funny and we laughed.

▶ **Use these words to write a complete simple sentence.**

7. Raul   his   teeth   brushes

_____

8. tree   the   climbed   Helene

_____

▶ **Revisit a piece of your writing. Edit the draft to make sure all simple sentences are used correctly.**

9

Connect to Writing: Using Simple Sentences

▶ **Read the selection and choose the best answer to each question.**

> *Brice wrote the following paragraph about cooking eggs. Read his paragraph and look for any revisions he should make. Then answer the questions that follow.*

(1) My dad and I cooked breakfast. (2) Eggs and bacon. (3) Cracked the eggs. (4) Dad sprinkled on salt and pepper. (5) Sizzled in the pan. (6) Then Dad and I. (7) The eggs were perfect. (8) Cooking breakfast was fun!

1. Every sentence needs a subject and a predicate. What is missing from sentence 3?

A. a subject

B. a predicate

C. a subject and a predicate

D. Nothing is missing.

2. What change, if any, should be made to sentence 6?

A. Add a subject, such as *eggs*.

B. Add a predicate, such as *added cheese*.

C. Add a subject and a predicate, such as *Mom pitched in, too*.

D. Make no change.

▶ **What do you like to eat for breakfast? Write two or three sentences about it.**

Statements and Questions

A **statement** is a sentence that tells something. A statement begins with a capital letter and ends with a period.

A **question** is a sentence that asks something. A question begins with a capital letter and ends with a question mark.

The tree is very tall.   How tall is the tree?

▶ **Write the correct end mark for each sentence.**

1. Marteice and her sister have three dolls _____

2. The chicken flapped its wings _____

3. Where is the museum _____

4. Is it my turn to play _____

5. Rain poured from the sky _____

6. Did you hear the news _____

7. The bananas are ripe _____

8. Will you read me a story _____

9. Why do dogs pant _____

10. Mr. Patel takes photos _____

▶ **Revisit a piece of your writing. Edit the draft to make sure all kinds of sentences are used correctly.**

Commands

> A **command** is a sentence that gives an order.
>
> A command begins with a capital letter and ends with a period.
>
> Pick up the jar of marbles.

▶ **Underline the sentence if it is a command.**

1. Bring me your hat.

2. You can take your sister to the store.

3. Jump over this branch.

4. The bees make honey.

5. Find the keys.

6. Keep your voice down.

7. It is windy.

8. The sun is going down.

9. Finish your homework.

10. Look at the moon.

▶ **Revisit a piece of your writing. Edit the draft to make sure commands are used correctly.**

Exclamations

> An **exclamation** is a sentence that shows strong feeling.
> An exclamation begins with a capital letter and ends with an exclamation point.
>
> That squirrel ate my peanut!

▶ **Write each exclamation correctly.**

1. My mom really liked my story

   _____

2. I found my lost watch

   _____

3. Our team won the game

   _____

4. That horse runs so fast

   _____

5. The light is too bright

   _____

▶ **Revisit a piece of your writing. Edit the draft to make sure exclamations are used correctly.**

Review Kinds of Sentences

> **Statement:** Meena plays chess.
>
> **Question:** Is Meena playing chess?
>
> **Command:** Follow the rules.
>
> **Exclamation:** Meena is the chess champion!

▶ **Write the correct end mark for each sentence.**

1. Look both ways before you cross the road _____

2. Can we go to the movies now _____

3. Will you help me pull weeds _____

4. That tasted delicious _____

▶ **Change each sentence to another kind of sentence. The word in ( ) tells what kind of sentence to write.**

5. Luci's mom is a school principal. (question)

_____

6. I want you to listen to me. (command)

_____

7. Did Angel finish the test first? (statement)

_____

▶ **Revisit a piece of your writing. Edit the draft to make sure all kinds of sentences are used correctly.**

_____

Connect to Writing: Using Different Kinds of Sentences

▶ Read the selection and choose the best answer to each question.

> *Raquel wrote the following paragraph about her pet rabbit. Read her paragraph and look for any revisions she should make. Then answer the questions that follow.*

(1) I have a pet rabbit. (2) Her name is Muffin Cup. (3) She is brown with white paws. (4) She twitches her nose when she snacks on a carrot. (5) She also likes to eat lettuce. (6) I clean her cage once each week. (7) I pet her soft fur. (8) Maybe I'll get another rabbit.

1. Every sentence in Raquel's paragraph is a statement. How could she rewrite sentence 7 to make her writing more interesting?

A. Is her fur soft?

B. Pet her soft fur.

C. Her fur is so soft!

D. Her fur is soft.

2. Which of the following questions could Raquel write to replace sentence 8?

A. Should I get another rabbit?

B. Is Muffin Cup hungry?

C. Does Muffin Cup want another snack?

D. Who will play with Muffin Cup?

▶ What kind of pet would you like? Write two or three sentences about it. Use different kinds of sentences.

Grade 2 · Kinds of Sentences

Compound Sentences with Conjunctions

A **compound sentence** is made up of two shorter sentences joined by **and**, **but**, or **or**.

A **comma** is used before the joining word.

I brought pineapple slices, **and** my sister brought potato salad.

▶ **Draw a line under the two shorter sentences in each compound sentence. Circle the joining word.**

1. No one wanted to leave, but it was getting late.

2. Runu woke up early, and she has to work late.

3. Trey started a campfire, and we all gathered around it.

4. Is that a frog, or is it a toad?

5. You can look at the moon, but don't look at the sun!

▶ **Revisit a piece of your writing. Edit the draft to make sure all compound sentences with conjunctions are used correctly.**

Forming Compound Sentences

A **compound sentence** is made up of two shorter sentences joined by **and**, **but**, or **or**.

A **comma** is used before the joining word.

I wanted a smoothie. The restaurant doesn't sell them.

I wanted a smoothie, **but** the restaurant doesn't sell them.

▶ **Write each pair of sentences as a compound sentence. Use a comma and a joining word.**

1. Some lizards live in the desert. Others live in tropical places.

   _____

2. It is hot during the day. It is cold at night

   _____

3. Have you seen a desert in person? Have you only seen pictures?

   _____

4. I wanted to be Mr. Romero's helper. He chose Shonda instead.

   _____

5. Take off your coat. Hang it in the closet.

   _____

▶ **Revisit a piece of your writing. Edit the draft to make sure all compound sentences are used correctly.**

_____

Combining Sentences

> A **compound sentence** is made up of two shorter sentences.
> The two shorter sentences are joined by **and**, **but**, or **or**.
> A **comma** is used before the joining word.
>
> Sari wants to take Lu for a walk. Lu is too tired.
> Sari wants to take Lu for a walk, **but** Lu is too tired.

▶ **Write each pair of sentences as a compound sentence.**

1. Most people had to wait in line. Molly had a special pass.

_____

2. We can go to the café. We can make breakfast at home.

_____

3. Xun met his favorite author. She signed a book for him.

_____

4. Lavonne needs change. I only have dollar bills.

_____

5. The mayor finished her speech. Everyone clapped

_____

▶ **Revisit a piece of your writing. Edit the draft to make sure all compound sentences are used correctly.**

Review Compound Sentences

A **compound sentence** is made up of two shorter sentences. The shorter sentences are connected by the word **and**, **but**, or **or**. Use a **comma** before the connecting word.

Short Sentences: I took snacks. Gia took water.
Compound Sentences: I took snacks, **and** Gia took water.

▶ **Draw a line under each compound sentence.**

1. Check the weather before a hike, or you might get rained on.

2. My job is to feed the pets and give them water.

3. Aiden picked apples, and we made a pie with them.

4. Would you like a salad, a sandwich, or soup for lunch?

5. The rain is making puddles. The street is wet.

6. We went to the shelter, and we adopted a dog.

7. The strawberries are sweet, but the grapes are sour.

8. I have a lot of paper, I need more pencils.

9. Hand me the book, or put it on the table.

10. The play was good, but it lasted too long.

▶ **Revisit a piece of your writing. Edit the draft to make sure all compound sentences are used correctly.**

Connect to Writing:
Using Compound Sentences

▶ **Read the selection and choose the best answer to each question.**

> *Lili wrote the following paragraph about going to the movies. Read her paragraph and look for any revisions she should make. Then answer the questions that follow.*

(1) Saturday we went to the movies. (2) I wanted to see a movie about pirates. (3) My brother wanted to see a movie about outer space. (4) My mother had to choose a movie. (5) She chose a funny movie. (6) We all really liked it.

1. Which sentence shows how to combine sentences 2 and 3?

A. I wanted to see a movie about pirates, my brother wanted to see a movie about outer space.

B. I wanted to see a movie about pirates, but my brother wanted to see a movie about outer space.

2. Which sentence shows how to combine sentences 5 and 6?

A. She chose a funny movie, and we all really liked it.

B. She chose a funny movie but we all really liked it.

▶ **What kind of movies do you like? Write two or three sentences about it. Include at least one compound sentence.**

_____

Grade 2 • Compound Sentences
© Houghton Mifflin Harcourt Publishing Company. All rights reserved.

Printable
20

Compound Subjects

A **compound subject** is formed by two or more nouns that make up the subject of a sentence. The nouns are joined by the word *and* or *or*.

Balloons and streamers hang from the ceiling.
Nathan or Bette will wrap the present.

▶ **Draw a line under each compound subject.**

1. Our cats and dogs play together.

2. The wind and rain kept us inside.

3. Mom or Dad will take me to practice.

4. My sister and I played a board game.

5. Pancakes or waffles are good for breakfast.

6. Rosa or I will win first place.

7. Jupiter and Saturn have many moons.

8. The sheets and towels get washed weekly.

9. Salt and pepper add flavor to food.

10. A squirrel or raccoon is in the attic!

▶ **Revisit a piece of your writing. Edit the draft to make sure compound subjects are used correctly.**

Using Coordinating Conjunctions

> **Compound subjects** are connected by **coordinating conjunctions** like *and* and *or*.

▶ **Circle each coordinating conjunction.**

1. Sharks and dolphins swim in the ocean.

2. Malia or Oliver clears the table after dinner.

3. Pizza or pasta sounds good for dinner.

4. Runners and walkers cross the finish line.

5. Tables and chairs are stacked in the hallway.

▶ **Revisit a piece of your writing. Edit the draft to make sure coordinating conjunctions are used correctly.**

Using Compound Predicates

> **Compound predicates** name two or more things the subject did or does. Like compound subjects, compound predicates are formed with a coordinating conjunction, such as *and* or *or*.

▶ **Combine each pair of sentences. Write a sentence with a compound predicate.**

1. Jani cleaned. Jani listened to music.

   _____

2. Koji packs his lunch. Koji buys his lunch.

   _____

3. The train stops often. The train starts often.

   _____

4. We can hike today. We can stay home today.

   _____

5. Aric flipped. Aric landed on his feet.

   _____

▶ **Revisit a piece of your writing. Edit the draft to make sure all coordinating conjunctions are used correctly.**

Review Compound Subjects and Predicates

A **compound subject** is formed by two or more nouns that make up the subject of a sentence. The nouns are joined by the coordinating conjunction *and* or *or*.

A **compound predicate** names two or more things the subject did or does. A compound predicate is also formed with a coordinating conjunction.

▶ **Read each sentence. Write S if it has a compound subject. Write P if it has a compound predicate.**

1. Bob and Fred found paper towels. _____

2. Alice made a salad and baked bread. _____

3. Theo plays soccer or rides his bike after school. _____

4. The principal or secretary can help us. _____

5. The shirt and pants match nicely. _____

6. Children swing or climb at the playground. _____

7. Mika watched the cartoon and laughed. _____

8. Matt and Jose ate cheese sandwiches. _____

9. Kahlil washed and dried all of the dishes. _____

10. Turtles and fish live in this pond. _____

▶ **Revisit a piece of your writing. Edit the draft to make sure compound subjects and predicates are used correctly.**

Connect to Writing: Using Compound Subjects and Predicates

▶ **Read the selection and choose the best answer to each question.**

> *Han wrote the following paragraph about summer fun. Read his paragraph and look for any revisions he should make. Then answer the questions that follow.*

(1) In the summer, I swim at the pool. (2) In the summer, I dive at the pool. (3) Family night is fun. (4) Mom swims with me. (5) Dad swims with me. (6) We pack a picnic and eat there. (7) Everyone has a good time!

1. Which sentence shows how to combine sentences 1 and 2?

A. In the summer, I swim and in the summer I dive at the pool.

B. I swim at the pool and I dive at the pool.

C. In the summer, I swim and dive at the pool.

D. In the summer, I swim at the pool or I dive.

2. Which sentence shows how to combine sentences 4 and 5?

A. Mom swims with Dad.

B. Mom and me swim and Dad swims with me.

C. Mom and Dad swim with me.

D. Mom swims with me with Dad.

▶ **What do you like to do in the summer? Write two or three sentences about it. Include a compound subject or predicate.**

Subject-Verb Agreement

In a sentence that tells about now, singular subjects use a verb that ends in **-s**.

The student <u>sits</u> in the classroom.

In a sentence that tells about now, plural subjects use a verb without the **-s**.

The students <u>sit</u> in the classroom.

▶ **Circle the correct verb. Then rewrite the sentence.**

1. Plants and trees (grow, grows) in the forest.

   _____

2. My friends (run, runs) to catch the bus.

   _____

3. Greta (look, looks) for her backpack.

   _____

4. Stars (light, lights) up the sky.

   _____

5. Dwayne (jump, jumps) to catch the ball.

   _____

▶ **Revisit a piece of your writing. Edit the draft to make sure the subject and verb agree in each sentence.**

Subjects and More Verbs

> In a sentence that tells about now, add -**es** to a verb that ends in
> -s, -sh, -ch, -tch, -z, or -x to match a singular subject.
>
> **The trucks pass** by. **The truck passes** by.
> **Parents watch** the game. **A parent watches** the game.
> **The workers mix** cement. **The worker mixes** cement.

▶ **Draw a line under each correct sentence.**

1. Harlan fix my bicycle.

   Harlan fixes my bicycle.

2. A fly buzzes by my ear.

   A fly buzz by my ear.

3. Coach Carr teaches us how to throw.

   Coach Carr teach us how to throw.

4. The dart misses the target.

   The dart miss the target.

5. Mom wash my muddy shoes.

   Mom washes my muddy shoes.

▶ **Revisit a piece of your writing. Edit the draft to make sure the
subject and verb agree in each sentence.**

Pronouns and Verbs

> If the pronoun *he, she,* or *it* is the subject of a sentence that tells about now, add *-s* or *-es* to the verb.   He **catches** the ball.
>
> If the pronoun *I, you, we,* or *they* is the subject of a sentence that tells about now, do not add *-s* or *-es* to the verb.   They **look** for the dog.

▶ **Circle the correct verb to match the subject. Then write the sentence.**

1. I (reach, reaches) for the ticket.

   _____

2. He (look, looks) very cold.

   _____

3. They (cheer, cheers) when we score.

   _____

4. You (tell, tells) the truth.

   _____

5. It (seem, seems) later than 6:00.

   _____

▶ **Revisit a piece of your writing. Edit the draft to make sure the subject and verb agree in each sentence.**

Review Subject-Verb Agreement

In a sentence that tells about now, add -es to a verb that ends
in -s, -sh, -ch, -tch, -z, or -x to match a singular subject.
If the pronoun he, she, or it is the subject of a sentence that tells
about now, add -s or -es to the verb.
If the pronoun I, you, we, or they is the subject of a sentence that
tells about now, do not add -s or -es to the verb.

▶ **Circle the correct verb to match the subject.**

1. Cows (graze, grazes) in the field.

2. She (pick, picks) out a funny movie.

3. The train (chug, chugs) down the tracks.

4. He (drink, drinks) orange juice every day.

5. Flowers (bloom, blooms) in the spring.

▶ **Underline the sentences that are written correctly.**

6. The student reads books in the library.

7. We laughs at the joke.

8. They walk around the block.

9. He mixes the paints.

10. I knows the best shortcut.

▶ **Revisit a piece of your writing. Edit the draft to make sure the**
subject and verb agree in each sentence.

Connect to Writing: Using Correct Subject-Verb Agreement

▶ **Read the selection and choose the best answer to each question.**

Zoey wrote the following paragraph about visiting a zoo. Read her paragraph and look for any revisions she should make. Then answer the questions that follow.

(1) I visit the zoo with Grandpa. (2) An elephant swings its trunk. (3) A giraffe eats leaves. (4) Monkeys swings in the trees. (5) On the way home we stops and get lunch. (6) I can't wait to visit the zoo again.

1. What change, if any, should be made in sentence 4?

A. Monkeys swing in the trees. **B.** Monkeys swinging in the trees.

C. Monkey swing in the trees. **D.** Make no change.

2. What change, if any, should be made in sentence 5?

A. On the way home we stops and get lunches.

B. On the way home we stop and gets lunch.

C. On the way home we stop and get lunch.

D. Make no change.

▶ **Have you visited a zoo? What did you see? Write two or three sentences about it.**

Nouns for People and Animals

A word that names a person or an animal is a **common noun**.
A noun can name one or more than one.
A **spider** spins a web.

▶ **Write the noun that names a person or an animal in each sentence.**

1. The child plays on the swings. _____

2. The girl runs around the track. _____

3. A cat sleeps in the box. _____

4. The boy eats his lunch. _____

5. A friend has a birthday. _____

6. A fish swims in the pond. _____

7. The goat jumped over the fence. _____

8. A bird sat on the branch. _____

9. A squirrel finds a nut. _____

10. My uncle picked a flower. _____

▶ **Revisit a piece of your writing. Edit the draft to make sure all nouns for people and animals are used correctly.**

Nouns for Places and Things

Not all nouns name people and animals.

Nouns also name places and things. These are also **common nouns**.

The family went to the **beach**.

▶ **Write the noun that names a place or thing in each sentence.**

1. The sheep waited in the barn. _____

2. The chef baked a pie. _____

3. The man went to the store. _____

4. The book belongs to Jim. _____

5. The girl made some soup. _____

6. My friend went to the party. _____

7. The tree is filled with birds. _____

8. Jane moved to the city. _____

9. The street is crowded with people. _____

10. Our neighbor bought a car. _____

▶ **Revisit a piece of your writing. Edit the draft to make sure all nouns for places and things are used correctly.**

Nouns for People, Animals, Places, and Things

▶ **Write the noun that names a person or an animal in each sentence.**

1. My aunt paints pictures. _____

2. That boy runs so fast! _____

3. The goat jumped onto a bench. _____

4. A whale rose out of the ocean. _____

5. The bird built a nest. _____

▶ **Write the noun that names a place or thing in each sentence.**

6. The visitor carries a suitcase. _____

7. The man puts on his hat. _____

8. The snow fell on the children. _____

9. The driver walks into the garage. _____

10. The horse trots down the road. _____

▶ **Revisit a piece of your writing. Edit the draft to make sure all nouns for people, animals, places, and things are used correctly.**

Review Nouns

> A noun is a word that names a person, an animal, a place, or a thing.
>
> | Nouns for People | Nouns for Animals | Nouns for Places | Nouns for Things |
> |---|---|---|---|
> | doctor | cow | library | rock |
> | grandmother | horse | school | phone |
> | boy | mouse | street | sink |

▶ **Underline the noun in each sentence. Tell whether it is a person, an animal, a place, or a thing.**

1. The dog is playful. _____

2. Who planted the tree? _____

3. Ana came home this morning. _____

4. The store is open late today. _____

5. Our teacher came in early. _____

6. The truck stopped suddenly. _____

7. Here is my bedroom. _____

8. The birds sang to each other. _____

9. Where is my pen? _____

10. A friend visited us yesterday. _____

▶ **Revisit a piece of your writing. Edit the draft to make sure all nouns are used correctly.**

Connect to Writing: Using Nouns

▶ **Read the selection and choose the best answer to each question.**

> *Jane wrote the following paragraph about baking cookies. Read her paragraph and look for any revisions she should make. Then answer the questions that follow.*

(1) I baked some cookies for a person. (2) First I mixed the ingredients together. (3) Then I rolled the dough into balls. (4) I put them in the oven to bake. (5) I took them out and let them cool. (6) I brought the cookies to a place. (7) Everyone liked them very much. (8) I think I will bake cookies more often!

1. Using exact nouns makes writing better. What change, if any, could improve sentence 1?

A. Replace person with a noun like *friend*.

B. Replace cookies with a noun like *cake*.

C. Replace person with a noun like *people*.

D. Make no change.

2. Which of the following could replace sentence 6 and make it clearer?

A. We brought the cookies to a place.

B. I brought things to a place.

C. I brought the cookies to school.

D. I brought them all.

▶ **Have you visited a zoo? What did you see? Write two or three sentences about it.**

One and More Than One

> A **singular noun** names one person, animal, place, or thing.
>
> A **plural noun** names more than one person, animal, place, or thing.
> Add **-s** to most nouns to make them plural.
>
> A **bird** sits in the nest. Two **birds** sit in the nest.

▶ **Decide if the underlined noun is singular or plural.**

1. Many <u>owls</u> have yellow eyes.   singular   plural

2. One <u>egg</u> hatched.   singular   plural

3. Four <u>ducks</u> quacked.   singular   plural

4. A <u>feather</u> fell to the ground.   singular   plural

5. The bird flaps both <u>wings</u>.   singular   plural

6. The <u>beak</u> is strong.   singular   plural

7. Put some <u>seeds</u> in the feeder.   singular   plural

8. The nest is made of <u>twigs</u>.   singular   plural

9. The <u>eagle</u> can see far.   singular   plural

10. The <u>birdhouse</u> is blue.   singular   plural

▶ **Revisit a piece of your writing. Edit the draft to make sure all nouns that name one and more than one are used correctly.**

Adding -s

Use **plural nouns** when you are talking about more than one.

Add **-s** to most nouns to name more than one.

Singular	Plural
My cat drank milk.	My cats drank milk.

▶ **Change the underlined noun into a plural noun. Write the new noun next to the sentence.**

1. The <u>cup</u> sat on the table. _____

2. The <u>sound</u> filled the room. _____

3. The <u>cat</u> jumped. _____

4. The <u>plate</u> fell to the floor. _____

5. The <u>swimmer</u> raced. _____

6. We moved the <u>chair</u>. _____

7. I picked up the <u>book</u>. _____

8. Carl lit the <u>candle</u>. _____

9. My <u>cousin</u> visited. _____

10. Lena found the <u>key</u>. _____

▶ **Revisit a piece of your writing. Edit the draft to make sure all nouns with -s are used correctly.**

Adding -s and -es

> Use **plural nouns** when you are talking about more than one.
>
> Add -**s** to most nouns to name more than one.
>
> Add -**es** to nouns that end with -s, -x, -ch, or -sh to name more than one.
>
> one fox   two foxes
>
> Two (fox, **foxes**) live in the woods.

▶ **Write the correct noun in each sentence. Reread each sentence to make sure that the noun makes sense.**

1. We planted a _____. (bush, bushes)

2. I washed two _____. (glass, glasses)

3. She packed four _____. (lunch, lunches)

4. Will you bake a _____ of cookies? (batch, batches)

5. We picked six _____. (peach, peaches)

6. I found two _____. (branch, branches)

7. We packed one _____. (box, boxes)

8. I made three _____. (wish, wishes)

9. He opened both _____. (latch, latches)

10. We got five free _____. (pass, passes)

▶ **Revisit a piece of your writing. Edit the draft to make sure all nouns with -s and -es are used correctly.**

Review Singular and Plural Nouns

> **Singular nouns** name one. **Plural nouns** name more than one.
>
> Add **-s** to most nouns to name more than one.
>
> Add **-es** to nouns that end with -s, -x, -ch, or -sh to name more than one.

▶ **Read each sentence. Underline a noun if it is singular, and circle a noun if it is plural.**

1. I put on my mittens.

2. She entered the race.

3. That is my bike.

4. We visited two parks.

5. I packed my bags.

▶ **Read each sentence. Add -s or -es to make the underlined noun plural.**

6. I bought two hat _____.

7. All the class _____ were outside.

8. We saw four finch _____.

9. I counted six boat _____ in the lake.

10. We played three game _____.

▶ **Revisit a piece of your writing. Edit the draft to make sure all singular and plural nouns are used correctly.**

Connect to Writing: Using Singular and Plural Nouns

▶ **Read the selection and choose the best answer to each question.**

> *Oscar wrote the following paragraph about a snowy day. Read his paragraph and look for any revisions he should make. Then answer the questions that follow.*

(1) It snowed yesterday. (2) There was snow everywhere! (3) Snow covered the tree branchs and roofs. (4) Truckes and cars were covered in snow, too. (5) We brought our sleds outside. (6) I rode down the hill very fast. (7) It was fun!

1. What change, if any, should be made in sentence 3?

A. Change *Snow* to *Snows*.

B. Change *branchs* to *branches*.

C. Change *roofs* to *roofes*.

D. Make no change.

2. What change, if any, should be made in sentence 4?

A. Change *Truckes* to *Trucks*.

B. Change *snow* to *snowes*.

C. Change *cars* to *cares*.

D. Make no change.

▶ **What would you do on a snowy day? What would it look like? Write two or three sentences about it.**

_____

_____

_____

Adding -*es* to Nouns

Add -**s** to most nouns to name more than one.

Add -**es** to nouns that end with -*s, -x, -ch,* or -*sh* to name more than one.

one lunch, two lunches

We made two (lunch, **lunches**).

▶ **Write the correct noun in each sentence. Reread each sentence to make sure that the noun makes sense.**

1. The house has a front _____. (porch, porches)

2. They lit two _____. (torch, torches)

3. I found an empty _____. (box, boxes)

4. Sara picked some _____. (peach, peaches)

5. They visited all our _____. (class, classes)

6. I picked up one _____. (dish, dishes)

7. He stood on this _____. (bench, benches)

8. She bought a _____. (watch, watches)

9. The grapes grow in _____. (bunch, bunches)

10. My cut needed three _____. (stitch, stitches)

▶ **Revisit a piece of your writing. Edit the draft to make sure all plural nouns with -*es* are used correctly.**

Nouns That Change Spelling

Some nouns change their spelling to name more than one.

one child   two children

Two (child, **children**) find a shell.

▶ **Write the correct noun to finish each sentence. Reread each sentence to make sure that it makes sense.**

1. Two _____ take a walk. (child, children)

2. I soaked both my _____. (foot, feet)

3. One _____ is in the pond. (goose, geese)

4. Many _____ stand near the hole. (man, men)

5. Four _____ ran under the porch. (mouse, mice)

6. A _____ stood at the bus stop. (person, people)

7. Two _____ waited in line. (woman, women)

8. I lost a _____. (tooth, teeth)

9. Six _____ flew over us. (goose, geese)

10. I hurt my left _____. (foot, feet)

▶ **Revisit a piece of your writing. Edit the draft to make sure all plural nouns that change spelling are used correctly.**

Collective Nouns

> A **collective noun** names a group of people or things.
> Our **class** reads about planets.

▶ **Draw a line under the collective noun in each sentence.**

1. There are six new players on our team.

2. I have a collection of stamps.

3. An army of ants marched in the sand.

4. The club has sixteen members.

5. We saw a flock of birds at the pond.

6. I knew many people in the crowd.

7. My friends were in the audience.

8. A herd of deer lives in this forest.

9. The family is going camping.

10. I met everyone in the group.

▶ **Revisit a piece of your writing. Edit the draft to make sure all collective nouns are used correctly.**

Review Plural Nouns

Nouns That Add -es	Nouns That Change Spelling	Collective Nouns
finches	children	class
boxes	mice	group
passes	feet	team

▶ **Add -s or -es to make each bold noun plural.**

1. **Fox** _____ have bushy tails.

2. All the **class** _____ went on the trip.

3. My brother has six **hat** _____.

4. I opened the **lock** _____.

▶ **Write the correct noun to complete each sentence.**

5. I met many _____ at the party. (person, people)

6. I kicked the ball with my right _____. (foot, feet)

7. I saw eight _____ in the park. (goose, geese)

▶ **Draw a line under the collective noun in each sentence.**

8. How many are in the group? 9. Members of our family live here.

10. A flock of birds landed in our yard.

▶ **Revisit a piece of your writing. Edit the draft to make sure all plural nouns are used correctly.**

Connect to Writing: Using Plural Nouns

▶ Read the selection and choose the best answer to each question.

> *Malia wrote the following paragraph about a picnic. Read her paragraph and look for any revisions she should make. Then answer the questions that follow.*

(1) Our club had a picnic on Saturday. (2) Sam brought boxs of dishes and cups. (3) I made 10 sandwiches. (4) Jordan made 2 batches of cookies. (5) We ate on a blanket in the park. (6) Some goose walked near us. (7) They wanted to share our food! (8) Later, we ran in the cool grass in bare feet.

1. What change, if any, should be made in sentence 2?

A. Change *boxs* to *boxes*.

B. Change *dishes* to *dishs*.

C. Change *cups* to *cup*.

D. Make no change.

2. What change, if any, should be made in sentence 6?

A. Change *Some goose* to *Some gooses*.

B. Change *Some goose* to *A flock of goose*.

C. Change *Some goose* to *Some geese*.

D. Make no change.

▶ Imagine you are going on a picnic. What would you bring? What would you do? Write two or three sentences about it.

_____

_____

Names for People, Animals, Places, and Things

Some **nouns** name special people, animals, places, or things. These special nouns are **proper nouns**. Proper nouns begin with capital letters.

Today **Jane Lee** paints a picture.

▶ **Write the proper nouns correctly.**

1. That girl is named maggie. _____

2. We took a trip to the grand canyon. _____

3. We visited ray ruiz. _____

4. They ate store-bought nana's kale chips. _____

5. I gave carrots to our rabbit fluffy. _____

6. We rode on the crazy loop coaster. _____

7. My grandmother lives in london. _____

8. The horse is named jumper. _____

9. Have you met kim miller? _____

10. We are going to the gardner museum. _____

▶ **Revisit a piece of your writing. Edit the draft to make sure all proper nouns are used correctly.**

Names for Special People and Animals

> Some **nouns** name special people or animals. These are **proper nouns**. Names for special people and animals begin with capital letters.
>
> **Maya** fed her cat **Smoky**.

▶ **Write the name for each special person or animal next to each sentence.**

1. The clines have a swing set in their yard. _____

2. My dog skippy is really friendly. _____

3. Our cat sandy likes to sit in the sun. _____

4. We made a cake for ed campbell. _____

5. I like playing catch with katie. _____

6. My hamster elvis stays up all night. _____

7. This is my cousin sam baker. _____

8. She named her horse sparkles. _____

9. I went to visit the smiths. _____

10. I like to brush my guinea pig wilson. _____

▶ **Revisit a piece of your writing. Edit the draft to make sure all proper nouns are used correctly.**

Names for Special Places and Things

Some **nouns** name special places and things. These are **proper nouns**. Names for special places and things begin with capital letters.

I bought some **Popsmart Popcorn** at **Shoptown**.

▶ **Use the proofreading mark ☰ for capital letter to show which special places and things should be capitalized.**

1. We learned that olives grow in italy.

2. My favorite game is rocket racer.

3. These apples came from washington.

4. My best friend lives on fulmer road.

5. They drank sunfresh juice.

6. She has a printfast printer.

7. I put on my jumpmore sneakers.

8. We are moving to canada.

9. I go to fernwood grammar school.

10. Sophie has the new powersmart phone.

Review Proper Nouns

> **Proper nouns** are the names of special people, animals, places, or things. Proper nouns begin with capital letters.

▶ **Use the proofreading mark ≡ for capital letter to show which special places and things should be capitalized.**

1. I walked my dog lucky.

2. We played on the gametime gamer.

3. My mom drives a pierce sedan.

4. Koalas live in australia.

5. I packed a supernutty bar in my lunch box.

6. The harpers are on my team.

7. The library is on pelham road.

8. My best friend is sanjay patel.

9. We visited victoria falls.

10. Jason brought his cat striper.

Connect to Writing: Using Proper Nouns

▶ **Read the selection and choose the best answer to each question.**

Sam wrote the following paragraph about a visit with his grandparents.
Read his paragraph and look for any revisions he should make. Then
answer the questions that follow.

(1) I went to visit my grandparents in New York City. (2) They have a big dog.
(3) We went to the top of the Empire State Building. (4) We walked around
Central Park. (5) My cousin ellen worth took me to three museums. (6) I
bought a Statue of Liberty crown for my sister. (7) She looks really silly in it.
(8) I hope I get to go back there again soon.

1. Using proper nouns helps make writing clearer and more specific. Which
of the following could replace sentence 2 to make it clearer?

A. Change it to *They have a Big
Dog*.

B. Change it to *They have a big dog
named tigger*.

C. Change it to *They have a big
dog named Tigger*.

D. Make no change.

2. What change, if any, could improve sentence 5?

A. Capitalize *Cousin*.

B. Capitalize *Ellen Worth*.

C. Capitalize *Museums*.

D. Make no change.

▶ **Describe someplace you have visited. Where did you go? Whom did you
meet? What did you see and do? Write two or three sentences about it.**

_____

Days of the Week

There are seven days in a week: Monday, Tuesday, Wednesday, Thursday, Friday, Saturday, and Sunday.

The names of the days of the week are **proper nouns** and they begin with **capital letters**.

Bonnie teaches swimming on **Tuesday**.

▶ **Write each sentence correctly.**

1. Ellie saw Pete last wednesday.

_____

2. Jessica has a piano lesson on tuesday.

_____

3. Jake mails Aunt Lucy a card on friday.

_____

4. We meet the first monday of each month.

_____

5. On saturday Anna sees her grandmother.

_____

▶ **Revisit a piece of your writing. Edit the draft to make sure names for days of the week are used correctly.**

Months

> The names of months are **proper nouns** and they begin with **capital letters**.
>
> | | | | |
> |---|---|---|---|
> | January | April | July | October |
> | February | May | August | November |
> | March | June | September | December |
>
> School starts in **September**.

▶ **Write each underlined word correctly.**

1. It snows a lot in january. _____

2. In june we will go swimming. _____

3. The school play is in april. _____

4. My favorite month is october. _____

5. In august I will visit my cousins. _____

6. It rains a lot in november. _____

7. Will february be cold again this year? _____

8. We plant our garden in march. _____

9. Our town has a big fair in may. _____

10. Next july we will go to the parade. _____

▶ **Revisit a piece of your writing. Edit the draft to make sure the names of months are used correctly.**

Holidays

> The names of holidays are **proper nouns** and they begin with **capital letters**.
>
> Thanksgiving   Labor Day   Independence Day
>
> We celebrate **Veterans Day** in November.

▶ **Write each underlined word or phrase correctly.**

1. We are very busy on <u>thanksgiving</u>. _____

2. We don't have school on <u>labor day</u>. _____

3. There is a parade on <u>memorial day</u>. _____

4. When is <u>presidents' day</u>? _____

5. We planted a tree on <u>arbor day</u>. _____

6. Did you know that <u>flag day</u> is in June? _____

7. The first day of January is <u>new year's day</u>. _____

8. Sylvie made a card for <u>mother's day</u>. _____

9. Will you watch fireworks on <u>independence day</u>? _____

10. People guess the weather on <u>groundhog day</u>. _____

▶ **Revisit a piece of your writing. Edit the draft to make sure the names of holidays are used correctly.**

_____

Review Using Proper Nouns

Proper nouns begin with **capital letters**. Each important word in the name of a holiday begins with a capital letter, too.

Days	Months	Holidays
Monday	March	New Year's Day
Friday	July	Thanksgiving Day
Sunday	September	Fourth of July

▶ **Write each sentence correctly.**

1. The pond often freezes in january.

   _____

2. Next wednesday is my birthday.

   _____

3. My grandmother visits on sunday.

   _____

4. The flowers bloom in april.

   _____

5. The independence day cookout was fun!

   _____

▶ **Revisit a piece of your writing. Edit the draft to make sure all proper nouns are used correctly.**

Connect to Writing: Using Proper Nouns

▶ **Read the selection and choose the best answer to each question.**

> *Nina wrote a paragraph about her favorite holiday. Read her paragraph and look for any revisions she should make. Then answer the questions.*

(1) My favorite holiday is thanksgiving day. (2) It takes place in november.
(3) I like it because my whole family comes over. (4) I play games with my
cousins. (5) We eat dinner. (6) At night we go to the movies. (7) I can't wait!

1. What change, if any, could improve sentence 1?

A. Replace holiday with Holiday.

B. Replace thanksgiving day with Thanksgiving Day.

C. Replace thanksgiving with Thanksgiving.

D. Make no change.

2. Using proper nouns that tell when can make your writing clearer. Which of the following could replace sentence 2 and make it clearer?

A. It takes place on a Thursday in November.

B. It takes place at noon on november.

C. It takes place on a day in november.

D. It takes place during November.

▶ **What is your favorite holiday? Why do you like it? What do you do on that holiday? Write two or three sentences about it.**

_____

_____

Nouns Ending with 's

A **possessive noun** shows that a person, animal, or thing owns or has something.

When a noun names one, add an **apostrophe (') and s** to that noun to show ownership. This makes the noun a possessive noun.

The **child's** blanket is soft.

▶ **Read each sentence. Underline the sentence that uses a possessive noun correctly.**

1. We see Trey's house.
   We see Treys house.

2. Don't sit on the tree's branches.
   Don't sit on the trees branches.

3. The donkeys ears are very long.
   The donkey's ears are very long.

4. Our teacher is Ben's aunt.
   Our teacher is Bens aunt.

5. We followed the games rules.
   We followed the game's rules.

6. That is my dogs bed.
   That is my dog's bed.

7. The phone's screen glows.
   The phones screen glows.

8. Mom's scarf is green.
   Moms scarf is green.

9. I found Petes gloves.
   I found Pete's gloves.

10. Jason spoke to the store's manager.
    Jason spoke to the stores manager.

▶ **Revisit a piece of your writing. Edit the draft to make sure all nouns ending with an -'s are used correctly.**

Nouns Ending with an Apostrophe

A **possessive noun** shows that a person, animal, or thing owns or has something.

When a noun names more than one and ends in -s, add just an **apostrophe (')** after the ending -s to show ownership.

The **musicians'** show was great.

▶ **Read each pair of sentences. Underline the sentence that uses a possessive noun correctly.**

1. The players' uniforms are new.
    The players uniforms are new.

2. We read the kids' books.
    We read the kids books.

3. The boys shoes were wet.
    The boys' shoes were wet.

4. All the clocks alarms went off.
    All the clocks' alarms went off.

5. The teachers' room is down the hall.
    The teachers room is down the hall.

6. We heard the girls' voices.
    We heard the girls voices.

7. The buildings lights sparkled.
    The buildings' lights sparkled.

8. My cousins cat is very friendly.
    My cousins' cat is very friendly.

9. The bees' hive is buzzing.
    The bees hive is buzzing.

10. The cars' engines roared.
    The cars engines roared.

▶ **Revisit a piece of your writing. Edit the draft to make sure all nouns ending with an apostrophe are used correctly.**

Forming Possessive Nouns

When a noun names one person or thing, add an **apostrophe (')** and an *s* to that noun to show ownership.

The <u>**singer's**</u> voice was loud.

When a noun names more than one and ends in -*s*, add just an **apostrophe (')** after the -*s* to show ownership.

The <u>**singers'**</u> voices were loud.

▶ **Underline the sentence that uses a possessive noun correctly.**

1. My bikes' front tire has a leak.
   My bike's front tire has a leak.

2. A bear's cubs played.
   A bears' cubs played.

3. The dogs' tails wagged.
   The dogs tails wagged.

4. The man's hat blew away.
   The mans' hat blew away.

5. The books covers were dusty.
   The books' covers were dusty.

▶ **Revisit a piece of your writing. Edit the draft to make sure all possessive nouns are used correctly.**

Review Possessive Nouns

Add an **apostrophe (')** and **s ('s)** to a singular noun to show ownership.

Add an apostrophe (') to a plural noun that ends in *-s* to show ownership.

Singular Possessive Nouns	Plural Possessive Nouns
one girl's shoe	five girls' shoes
a town's festival	many towns' festivals

▶ **Write the possessive form of each underlined singular noun.**

1. The <u>fish</u> food floats in the water. _____

2. We went to my <u>aunt</u> house. _____

3. The <u>sink</u> drain is clogged. _____

4. Do you know the <u>store</u> hours? _____

5. The <u>chef</u> hat is tall and white. _____

▶ **Write the possessive form of each underlined plural noun.**

6. We listened to the <u>birds</u> songs. _____

7. Our <u>cousins</u> farm is in Iowa. _____

8. All the <u>artists</u> pictures were colorful. _____

9. The <u>nurses</u> uniforms are blue. _____

10. Hang <u>visitors</u> coats in the closet. _____

▶ **Revisit a piece of your writing. Edit the draft to make sure all possessive nouns are used correctly.**

Connect to Writing: Using Possessive Nouns

▶ **Read the selection and choose the best answer to each question.**

> Sara wrote a paragraph about a surprise from her cousins. Read her paragraph. Look for any revisions she should make. Then answer the questions.

(1) I have two cousins named Amy and Lea. (2) My cousins house is a block away from mine. (3) One day they told me to come over. (4) They had a surprise. (5) It was a dog! (6) A friend of my aunt named Kim helps animals who need homes. (7) She thought this dog would be perfect for Amy and Lea. (8) She was right!

1. What change, if any, could improve sentence 2?

A. Change *My cousins house* to *My cousins' house.*

B. Change *My cousins house* to *My cousin's house.*

C. Change *My cousins house* to *Cousins house.*

D. Change *My cousins house* to *Their cousins house.*

2. Which of the following could replace sentence 6 to make it less wordy?

A. A friend of my aunt's named Kim helps animals who need homes.

B. A friend of my aunt's, helps animals and finds them homes.

C. My aunt's friend Kim helps animals who need homes.

D. Kim, who is a friend of my aunt's, finds animals homes to help them.

▶ **Describe a time when you were surprised by something. What made it a surprise? Write two or three sentences about it.**

_____

_____

Subject Pronouns

The **subject** of a sentence names the person or thing that does the action. A **pronoun** can take the place of this noun.

Greg is sick at home   Subject: Greg

He is sick at home.   Pronoun: He

▶ **Write the pronoun that can take the place of the underlined subject. Use the words in the Word Bank to help you.**

| He | She | It | They |

1. <u>Marissa</u> has an idea for a project.

   _____ has an idea for a project.

2. <u>The students</u> paint a mural.

   _____ paint a mural.

3. <u>Mr. Stevens</u> gives the students paint and brushes.

   _____ gives the students paint and brushes.

4. <u>The mural</u> makes everyone smile.

   _____ makes everyone smile.

5. <u>Marissa and her friends</u> did a great job.

   _____ did a great job.

▶ **Revisit a piece of your writing. Edit the draft to make sure subject pronouns are used correctly.**

Object Pronouns

A **pronoun** can replace a noun that comes after a verb.

Use the pronouns *me, him, her, it, us,* and *them*.

Nouns	Pronouns
Esteban rode the **bike**.	Esteban rode **it**.
I saw **Annika** this morning	I saw **her** this morning.
Please help **my sisters**.	Please help **them**.

▶ **Write the pronoun that can take the place of the underlined word or words.**

1. Ms. Liu made the costumes.

   Ms. Liu made _____.

2. Conner handed Antonio a cape.

   Conner handed _____ a cape.

3. Aarti will wear the crown.

   Aarti will wear _____.

4. Ms. Liu asked Gina and me to try on the masks.

   Ms. Liu asked _____ to try on the masks.

5. We put the wings on Trisha.

   We put the wings on _____.

▶ **Revisit a piece of your writing. Edit the draft to make sure object pronouns are used correctly.**

Reflexive Pronouns

Reflexive pronouns refer back to the subject of the sentence. Examples of reflexive pronouns include *myself, yourself, himself, herself, ourselves,* and *themselves*.

Subject	Reflexive Pronoun	
I	ate breakfast by	**myself**.
We	ate breakfast by	**ourselves**.
He	ate breakfast by	**himself**.

▶ **Write the reflexive pronoun from the Word Bank that completes each sentence.**

myself	yourself	himself
herself	ourselves	themselves

1. Megan and I had a picnic by _____.

2. I braid my hair by _____.

3. Can you pour the milk _____?

4. Tucker and Mia paid for the tickets _____.

5. Isaiah makes his bed by _____.

▶ **Revisit a piece of your writing. Edit the draft to make sure reflexive pronouns are used correctly.**

Review Pronouns

> A **pronoun** can stand for a noun.
>
> These pronouns can replace the subject of a sentence: *I, he, she, it, we, they*.
>
> These pronouns come after a verb: *me, him, her, it, us, them*.
>
> These **reflexive pronouns** come after a verb: *myself, yourself, himself, herself, ourselves, themselves*.

▶ **Write the pronoun that can replace the underlined words. Choose from the Word Bank.**

> she   us   it   him   themselves

1. Bella is on the swings. _____

2. I like to play with Pankaj. _____

3. Kick the ball to Damian and me. _____

4. The light is too bright. _____

5. Mia and Alex made a fort for Mia and Alex. _____

▶ **Revisit a piece of your writing. Edit the draft to make sure all pronouns are used correctly.**

Connect to Writing: Using Pronouns

▶ **Read the selection and choose the best answer to each question.**

> *Isabela wrote the following paragraph about a special family dinner. Read her paragraph and look for any revisions she should make. Then answer the questions that follow.*

(1) My parents work very hard. (2) My sister and I made dinner to surprise them. (3) I made a salad all by myself. (4) My big sister made rice all by myself. (5) My big sister also made a chicken dish. (6) Next time, we'll make breakfast.

1. What change should be made to sentence 4?

A. Change *My big sister* to *Her*.

B. Change *myself* to *me*.

C. Change *My big sister* to *We*.

D. Change *myself* to *herself*.

2. What change should be made to sentence 5 to prevent repeated nouns?

A. Change *My big sister* to *She*.

B. Change *My big sister* to *Her*.

C. Change *My big sister* to *Herself*.

D. Change *My big sister* to *We*.

▶ **When did you do something to help others? Did you do it all by yourself? Write two or three sentences about it.**

_____

_____

_____

_____

Pronouns and Ownership

A **possessive pronoun** shows that a person or an animal owns or has something.

My, *your*, *his*, *her*, and *their* come before a noun to show that someone has or owns something.

<u>My</u> brother has two trophies.

▶ **Underline the possessive pronoun in each sentence. Circle the noun that goes with it.**

1. My dad is washing his car.

2. I lost my homework.

3. May I borrow your eraser?

4. Gloria wore her boots today.

5. I saw their boat on the lake.

▶ **Revisit a piece of your writing. Edit the draft to make sure possessive pronouns are used correctly.**

More Pronouns and Ownership

Some **possessive pronouns** stand alone. They are usually at the end of a sentence.

Mine, yours, his, hers, and *theirs* are possessive pronouns that come after nouns.

Which backpack is **yours**?

▶ **Underline the possessive pronoun in each sentence. Circle the noun that shows what is owned.**

1. That fork is hers.

2. This plate is mine.

3. The blue napkin is his.

4. Which glass is yours?

5. The small bowls are theirs.

▶ **Revisit a piece of your writing. Edit the draft to make sure possessive pronouns are used correctly.**

Possessive Pronouns

A **possessive pronoun** shows that a person or animal owns or has something.

Some **possessive pronouns** come right before a noun.

<u>My</u> blanket is soft.

Some **possessive pronouns** stand alone. They are usually at the end of a sentence.

<u>The</u> blanket is **mine**.

▶ **Underline the possessive pronoun in each sentence. Circle the noun that goes with it.**

1. Are those your sunglasses?

2. The white dog is mine.

3. Ang is my cousin.

4. That hamster is his.

5. Naomi is her friend.

▶ **Revisit a piece of your writing. Edit the draft to make sure possessive pronouns are used correctly.**

Review Possessive Pronouns

Possessive pronouns show that something belongs to someone.
The pronouns *my, your, his, her,* and *their* come before a noun.
The pronouns *mine, yours, his, hers,* and *theirs* come at the end of
a sentence.

▶ **Circle the possessive pronoun in each sentence. Underline the noun that goes with it.**

1. That green shirt is mine.

2. The small bag is yours.

3. Their sign is the biggest.

4. Anna showed the medal to her class.

5. I couldn't believe my eyes.

6. Hugo said the chalk is his.

7. Is that notebook hers?

8. Can you bring your camera?

9. My camera is broken.

10. Marina hung her mirror on the wall.

▶ **Revisit a piece of your writing. Edit the draft to make sure possessive pronouns are used correctly.**

Connect to Writing: Using Possessive Pronouns

▶ **Read the selection and choose the best answer to each question.**

> *Dalip wrote a paragraph about being given a tool. Read his paragraph and look for any revisions he should make. Then answer the questions.*

(1) My dad bought two new hammers. (2) Dad got a toolbox from Dad's shed. (3) Dad gave me his old red hammer and gave my brother his old black hammer. (4) Niran picked up my red hammer. (5) I said, "That hammer is the one that belongs to me."

1. What change should be made to sentence 2 so that possessive nouns are not being repeated?

A. Dad got Dad's toolbox from his shed.

B. Dad got a toolbox from mine shed.

C. Dad got a toolbox from his shed.

D. Make no change.

2. What change should be made to sentence 5?

A. I said, "That one is my."

B. I said, "That hammer is yours."

C. I said, "That hammer is mine."

D. Make no change.

▶ **Have you been given something that belonged to someone else? Is there something you would like to be given? Write two or three sentences about it. Use possessive pronouns.**

_____

_____

_____

Grade 2 • Possessive Pronouns

Printable
70

Action Verbs

A **verb** names an action that someone or something does or did.

The rocket **moves** fast.

▶ **Underline the verb in each sentence.**

1. Astronauts climb onboard.

2. The engines start with a roar.

3. The excited crowd cheers loudly.

4. The countdown begins.

5. Scientists watch carefully.

6. The moment finally arrives!

7. The spacecraft blasts into the sky.

8. Reporters take pictures of the big event.

9. The rocket disappears above the clouds.

10. Everyone drives home from the launch site.

▶ **Revisit a piece of your writing. Edit the draft to make sure action verbs are used correctly.**

Action Verbs and Subjects

A **verb** tells what someone or something does or did. The **subject** tells who or what is doing the action.

(Mr. Gonzales) **trains** dogs.

▶ **Read each sentence. The verb is underlined. Circle the subject.**

1. Sparky <u>sits</u> on command.

2. The beagle <u>wags</u> its tail.

3. Puppies <u>chew</u> their toys.

4. I <u>want</u> a golden retriever.

5. A rabbit <u>teases</u> the dogs.

▶ **Read each sentence. The subject is circled. Underline the verb.**

6. The (collar) fits Spot perfectly.

7. (Kipper) begs for a treat.

8. My (dog) greets me at the door.

9. (I) scratch behind Tippy's ears.

10. The dog's (tags) jingle when it drinks.

▶ **Revisit a piece of your writing. Edit the draft to make sure action verbs and subjects are used correctly.**

Action Verbs in Sentences

> Verbs that tell about actions that happen now are called **present-tense verbs**.
> Verbs that tell about actions that happened before now are called **past-tense verbs**.

▶ **Underline the verb in each sentence. Circle whether the verb is in the present tense or in the past tense.**

1. The frogs croak.   present   past

2. Tadpoles wiggled in the pond.   present   past

3. We row our boat.   present   past

4. Jenny swings on a rope.   present   past

5. She dropped into the water.   present   past

6. Turtles crawl on the shore.   present   past

7. Greg watches for fish.   present   past

8. Ducks paddled their feet.   present   past

9. Plants floated on the water.   present   past

10. Otters dive for food.   present   past

▶ **Revisit a piece of your writing. Edit the draft to make sure action verbs are used correctly.**

Review Action Verbs

A **verb** names an action that someone or something does or did. A verb is found in the action part, or **predicate**, of a sentence.

▶ **Underline the verb in each sentence.**

1. Kimiko shuffles the cards.

2. They stacked the blocks.

3. Will someone play checkers with me?

4. The jump rope spins around and around.

5. Lionel moved his marker around the game board.

6. Mom and I sorted all of the puzzle pieces.

7. Kwan keeps score.

8. Two dice rolled across the table.

9. Mario guessed the correct letters.

10. Druve wins again!

▶ **Revisit a piece of your writing. Edit the draft to make sure action verbs are used correctly.**

Connect to Writing: Using Action Verbs

▶ Read the selection and choose the best answer to each question.

> Frank wrote the following paragraph about nighttime. Read his paragraph and look for any revisions he should make. Then answer the questions that follow.

(1) The sky grew dark. (2) I ran outside. (3) I saw some stars. (4) Then I saw the moon. (5) My cat was next to me. (6) Mom told me to get a jacket. (7) I counted the stars in the night sky. (8) There were too many to count!

1. Using exact verbs makes writing better. What change, if any, could improve sentence 2?

A. Replace *I* with *Frank*.　　**B.** Replace *ran* with *raced*.

C. Replace *outside* with *outdoors*.　　**D.** Make no change.

2. Which of the following could replace sentence 5 to make it more interesting?

A. The cat was beside me.　　**B.** My cat was next to something.

C. My cat cuddled next to me.　　**D.** My cat went next to me.

▶ **Have you ever looked at the night sky? What did you see happening? Write two or three sentences about it.**

_____

_____

Adding -s to Verbs

A **verb** can name an action that is happening now, or in the **present**.
Add -s to this kind of verb when it tells about a noun that names one.

The **bird** eats.   The **birds** eat.

▶ **Circle the correct present-tense verb in each sentence.**

1. The children (plant, plants) seeds.

2. Henri (dig, digs) in the dirt.

3. A hawk (sit, sits) in the tree.

4. Suzanne (cut, cuts) the grass.

5. Mom and Dad (pull, pulls) weeds together.

6. Cool water (spray, sprays) from the hose.

7. Clinton (rake, rakes) leaves into a pile.

8. Squirrels (gather, gathers) nuts.

9. Carmela (trim, trims) the bushes.

10. All of the neighbors (stay, stays) busy.

▶ **Revisit a piece of your writing. Edit the draft to make sure verbs in the present tense are used correctly.**

Adding -es to Verbs

A **verb** can tell about an action that is happening now. Add -es
to this kind of verb if it ends with -s, -x, -z, -ch, or -sh and if it tells
about a noun that names one.

A **coyote** pass<u>es</u> through the woods.
Coyotes pass through the woods.

▶ **Circle the correct present-tense verb in each sentence.**

1. A forest ranger (fix, fixes) the broken bridge.

2. Hikers (watch, watches) birds and other animals.

3. A fox (rush, rushes) to its den.

4. Mushrooms (push, pushes) out of the ground.

5. The bear (relax, relaxes) in the sun.

6. A raccoon (wash, washes) its food.

7. Baby bunnies (toss, tosses) and turn in their nest.

8. The bird (reach, reaches) for a twig.

9. An eagle (clutch, clutches) its prey.

10. Snakes (hiss, hisses) at a predator.

▶ **Revisit a piece of your writing. Edit the draft to make sure verbs
in the present tense are used correctly.**

Verbs with -s and -es

A **verb** can tell about an action that is happening now. When this kind of verb tells about a noun that names one, add -s to the verb. If the verb ends with -s, -x, -z, -ch, or -sh and tells about a noun that names one, add -es to the verb.

▶ **Draw a line under the verb that completes each sentence correctly.**

1. A cake (bake, bakes) in the oven.

2. Water (boil, boils) on the stove.

3. Food (chill, chills) in the freezer.

4. The toaster (sit, sits) on the counter.

5. Fruit (ripen, ripens) in the basket.

▶ **Write the verb correctly to go with the naming part of the sentence.**

6. Quon _____ the batter. (mix)

7. The dog _____ popcorn in her mouth. (catch)

8. Celine _____ to the table. (rush).

9. Leon _____ the pots and pans. (wash)

10. Dad _____ me the pepper. (pass)

▶ **Revisit a piece of your writing. Edit the draft to make sure verbs in the present tense are used correctly.**

Name _____

Review Verbs in the Present

Some **verbs** tell about actions that happen now, in the **present**. Add -s to this kind of verb when it tells about a noun that names one. Add -es to this kind of verb if it ends with -s, -x, -z, -ch, or -sh and it tells about a noun that names one.

▶ **Draw a line under the correct present-tense verb.**

1. The doctor (listen, listens) to my heart.

2. A nurse (take, takes) my temperature.

3. The office (smell, smells) clean.

4. The bandage (stick, sticks) to my skin.

5. Ms. Jung (give, gives) me a sticker.

▶ **Write the verb correctly to go with the naming part of the sentence.**

6. The hospital _____ with activity. (buzz)

7. Mr. Ziola _____ up the volunteers. (match)

8. A driver washes and _____ the ambulance. (wax)

9. Dr. Tiwar _____ her shift. (finish)

10. Ronin _____ the elevator button. (press)

▶ **Revisit a piece of your writing. Edit the draft to make sure verbs in the present tense are used correctly.**

Grade 2 • Verbs in the Present

Connect to Writing: Using Present-Tense Verbs

▶ **Read the selection and choose the best answer to each question.**

> *Raul wrote a paragraph about animals in the woods. Read his paragraph and look for any revisions he should make. Then answer the questions.*

(1) Many animals makes their home in the woods. (2) A bee buzzes near its hive. (3) A deer drinks from a pond. (4) A deer eats from the ground. (5) Robins fly from tree to tree. (6) Skunks dig for grubs. (7) A bear looks for good berries to eat.

1. What change, if any, should be made in sentence 1?

A. Change *animals* to *animal*.

B. Change *makes* to *make*.

C. Change *home* to *homes*.

D. Make no change.

2. Joining two shorter sentences with the same subject makes writing smoother. How can sentences 3 and 4 be joined to make the writing better?

A. A deer drinks from a pond, while the bear looks for good berries.

B. The deer drinks from and eats from the ground.

C. A deer eats from the ground, and robins fly from tree to tree.

D. A deer drinks from a pond and eats from the ground.

▶ **What do you know about animals that live in the woods? Write two or three sentences about it.**

_____

_____

Past-Tense Verbs with -ed

Some **verbs** name actions that are happening now, or in the **present**. Other verbs name actions that happened before now, or in the **past**. Add -ed to most verbs to show that the action happened in the past.

Yesterday we **visited** the farm.

▶ **Read each sentence. Draw a line under the verb that tells about the past.**

1. Hank (pass, passed) by the field.

2. Corn (swayed, sway) in the breeze.

3. Cows (blink, blinked) their large eyes.

4. The tractor (started, start) to move.

5. The ducks (quacked, quack) loudly.

6. Pigs (roll, rolled) in the mud.

7. Horses (pound, pounded) their hooves.

8. Chickens (scratched, scratch) at the ground.

9. The farmer (worked, work) hard.

10. Our family (paint, painted) the barn.

▶ **Revisit a piece of your writing. Edit the draft to make sure past-tense verbs are used correctly.**

Verbs in the Future Tense

Some **verbs** name actions that are going to happen. Add *will* before a verb to show that the action is going to happen in the **future**.

The birds **build** their nest.   **Present**
The birds **will build** their nest.   **Future**

▶ **Read each sentence. Draw a line under the verb that tells about the future.**

1. Dandelions (bloom, will bloom) in the field.

2. The crows (come, will come) out to eat.

3. Squirrels (will play, play) in the trees.

4. Wind (will blow, blow) the leaves.

5. Pinecones (fall, will fall) from the trees.

6. Ants (will crawl, crawl) over the ground.

7. Water birds (wade, will wade) in the pond.

8. Frogs (jump, will jump) away.

9. We (will collect, collect) rocks.

10. The sun (sets, will set) soon.

▶ **Revisit a piece of your writing. Edit the draft to make sure verbs in the future tense are used correctly.**

Present, Past, and Future Tense

Some **verbs** name actions that are happening now. Those verbs tell about the **present**. Some verbs name actions that happened before now, or in the **past**. Add -ed to most verbs to show that the action happened in the past. Some verbs name actions that are going to happen. Add will before a verb to show that the action is going to happen in the **future**.

▶ **Read each sentence. Underline the verb in each sentence. Then, change the verb so it is the tense shown in parentheses.**

1. The hungry zoo animals want food. (past) _____

2. The elephants moved their trunks. (present) _____

3. The lions roar loudly. (past) _____

4. Sea lions dance on their flippers. (future) _____

5. Giraffes stretch their necks. (future) _____

6. Penguins waddle back and forth. (past) _____

7. Eagles flapped their wide wings. (present) _____

8. Monkeys peeled bananas. (present) _____

9. Turtles nibbled on lettuce. (future) _____

10. We enjoy the zoo. (past) _____

▶ **Revisit a piece of your writing. Edit the draft to make sure verb tenses are used correctly.**

Review Verbs in the Present, Past, and Future

> Some **verbs** name actions that are happening now, or in the **present**. Some verbs name actions that happened before, or in the **past**. Other verbs name actions that will happen later, or in the **future**.
>
> | Present | Past | Future |
> |---|---|---|
> | The boats float. | The boats floated. | The boats will float. |
> | We watch them. | We watched them. | We will watch them. |

▶ **Circle the verb tense that tells when the action is happening in each sentence.**

1. Marisa likes the playground.   present   past   future

2. Bart jumped in the sandbox.   present   past   future

3. The twins will ride their bikes.   present   past   future

4. A train whistle blows.   present   past   future

5. Bree will meet us there.   present   past   future

6. Gus packs a lunch.   present   past   future

7. The seesaw tilted up and down.   present   past   future

8. Cecile climbed up the slide.   present   past   future

9. They push us on the swings.   present   past   future

10. Lia will come again tomorrow.   present   past   future

▶ **Revisit a piece of your writing. Edit the draft to make sure verb tenses are used correctly.**

Connect to Writing: Using Verbs in the Present, Past, and Future

▶ **Read the selection and choose the best answer to each question.**

> *Zhin wrote the following story about what she and a friend found in a field. Read her story and look for any revisions she should make. Then answer the questions that follow.*

(1) Leo and I walked through the field. (2) Leo pointed to something shiny. (3) We rushed over to see what it was. (4) Leo picks up a coin. (5) We looked at both sides. (6) We wondered how the coin got there. (7) Maybe a bird drops it!

1. Using verbs that tell about the same time makes writing easier to understand. Which change should be made in sentence 4 to make the story easier to understand?

A. Change *picks* to *will pick*.   **B.** Change *picks* to *picked*.

C. Change *picks* to *pick*.   **D.** Make no change.

2. What change, if any, should be made to sentence 7?

A. Change *drops* to *dropped*.   **B.** Change *drops* to *will drop*.

C. Change *drops* to *drop*.   **D.** Make no change.

▶ **Have you ever found something interesting? Write two or three sentences about it.**

_____

_____

_____

Using *Am, Is,* and *Are*

The verb *be* takes different forms. *Am, is,* and *are* tell about something happening now. Make sure the form of *be* agrees with the subject.

Use **am** with I.	**I am** excited.
Use **is** with one.	The **race is** starting.
Use **are** with more than one.	The **runners are** on the track.

▶ **Read each sentence. Draw a line under the correct verb.**

1. The runners (is, are) ready.

2. Fans (is, are) cheering them on.

3. I (am, is) rooting for my sister.

4. Coach Klay (is, are) watching.

5. The starter (is, are) sounding the horn.

▶ **Revisit a piece of your writing. Edit the draft to make sure the verb *be* is used correctly.**

Using *Was* and *Were*

> The verb *be* takes different forms. *Was* and *were* tell about something that happened in the past. Make sure the form of *be* agrees with the subject.
>
> | Use **was** with one. | The **train was** late. |
> |---|---|
> | Use **were** with more than one. | The **passengers were** annoyed. |

▶ **Read each sentence. Draw a line under the correct verb.**

1. The subway station (was, were) crowded.

2. Marina and Taji (was, were) waiting in line.

3. Wesley (was, were) on his way home.

4. A door (was, were) stuck shut.

5. Riders (was, were) sitting and standing in the train.

▶ **Revisit a piece of your writing. Edit the draft to make sure the verb *be* is used correctly.**

Using Forms of the Verb *Be*

> The verb *be* is a state of being verb.
>
> The present-tense forms of *be* are *am, is,* and *are.*
>
> The past-tense forms of *be* are *was* and *were.*

▶ **Read each sentence. Draw a line under the correct verb.**

1. The book fair (am, is, are) starting today.

2. My class (am, is, are) excited.

3. The books (was, were) all on a table.

4. There (am, is, are) so many different topics!

5. Frances (am, is, are) looking for a book on history.

6. I (am, is, are) looking for one about cats.

7. Mike (was, were) looking at a book about horses.

8. Teachers (was, were) buying books for their classrooms.

9. Dad said I (am, is, are) allowed to choose two books.

10. Clem and Josie (am, is, are) done shopping.

▶ **Revisit a piece of your writing. Edit the draft to make sure the verb *be* is used correctly.**

Review the Verb *Be*

> The verbs *am, is,* and *are* tell about something that is happening now.
> The verbs *was* and *were* tell about something that happened in the
> past. Use *am, is,* or *was* if the sentence tells about one noun. Use *are* or
> *were* if the sentence tells about more than one.

▶ **Choose the correct verb to complete each sentence. Write the verb on
the line.**

1. The soccer field _____ large. (am, is, are)

2. I _____ in the goal. (am, is, are)

3. The referees _____ helpful. (am, is, are)

4. Tyrell _____ put in the game. (was, were)

5. Zara and Pete _____ wearing uniforms. (was, were)

6. Rory's dog _____ chasing the ball. (am, is, are)

7. My shin guards _____ under my socks. (am, is, are)

8. Coach Darren said I _____ fast and strong. (am, is, are)

9. The ball _____ black and white. (was, were)

10. The snacks _____ delicious! (was, were)

▶ **Revisit a piece of your writing. Edit the draft to make sure the verb *be*
is used correctly.**

Connect to Writing: Using the Verb *Be*

▶ **Read the selection and choose the best answer to each question.**

> *Stella wrote the following paragraph about an event. Read her paragraph and look for any revisions she should make. Then answer the questions.*

(1) The theater is a busy place. (2) The actors are excited. (3) The actors are ready. (4) People are finding their seats. (5) Maya is reading the program. (6) The director were checking the props. (7) Roger is turning down the lights. (8) Everyone watches the curtain rise.

1. Joining two shorter sentences with the same subject and verb makes writing smoother. Which is the correct way to combine sentences 2 and 3?

A. The actors are excited and they ready.

B. The actors are excited and ready.

C. The actors are excited, ready.

D. The excited and ready actors.

2. Which sentence uses an incorrect form of the verb *be*?

A. Sentence 3

B. Sentence 4

C. Sentence 6

D. Sentence 8

▶ **What do you know about plays or the theater? Write two or three sentences about it.**

_____

_____

_____

Name _____

Grammar
3.5.1

Have, Has, and Had

Have, has, and had are **irregular verbs**. Use have and has to tell about present time. Use had to tell about something that happened in the past.

Subject	Present	Past
Johan and Maria I, We, You, They	have	had
Doris He, She, It	has	had

▶ **Circle the verb that correctly completes each sentence.**

1. Caryn (have, has) a ballet recital tonight.

2. The dancers (had, have) practice last week.

3. Stan and Lara (has, have) art class.

4. The paintbrush (have, has) a red handle.

5. Jeremy (had, have) a riding lesson yesterday.

6. Horses (have, has) long tails and manes.

7. You (has, have) nice bowling shoes.

8. My old bowling ball (have, had) swirls on it.

9. Luisa (has, have) a yellow belt in karate.

10. I (has, have) the same karate teacher.

▶ **Revisit a piece of your writing. Edit the draft to make sure the verbs have, has, and had are used correctly.**

Grade 2 • Irregular Verbs
© Houghton Mifflin Harcourt Publishing Company. All rights reserved.
Printable
91

Do, Does, and Did

Do, does, and did are **irregular verbs**. Use do and does to tell about present time. Use did to tell about something that happened in the past.

Subject	Present	Past
Zane and Mari I, We, You, They	do	did
Hilda He, She, It	does	did

▶ **Circle the verb that correctly completes each sentence.**

1. Last week Han (do, did) some exercises.

2. We (do, does) a lot of jumping jacks.

3. Chloe (do, does) push-ups on the mat.

4. Yesterday I (do, did) some stretches.

5. We (do, does) cartwheels.

6. Leona (do, does) gymnastics.

7. It (do, did) help to warm up first.

8. Yoga (do, does) build muscle.

9. Kiran and I (do, does) lunges.

10. Ms. Basu (do, did) 15 laps around the track.

▶ **Revisit a piece of your writing. Edit the draft to make sure the verbs do, does, and did are used correctly.**

Irregular Verbs

> The verbs *have* and *has* tell about the present. The verb *had* tells about the past.
> The verbs *do* and *does* tell about the present. The verb *did* tells about the past.

▶ **Underline the verb that correctly completes each sentence.**

1. Yesterday we (have, had) a nice lunch.

2. The plates (have, has) crumbs on them.

3. Jonah (do, does) the dishes.

4. He (has, have) chores each day.

5. I (do, did) my homework with Callie yesterday.

6. She and I (has, have) math class together.

7. Will you (do, did) me a favor?

8. It (has, have) to be done quickly.

9. Meena (do, does) yard work for her neighbors.

10. They (has, have) a lawn mower.

▶ **Revisit a piece of your writing. Edit the draft to make sure irregular verbs are used correctly.**

Review Irregular Verbs

The verbs *have, has, had, do, does,* and *did* are irregular verbs.

Subject	Present	Past
One	has, does	had, did
More Than One	have, do	had, did

▶ **Choose the verb that correctly completes each sentence. Write the verb on the line.**

1. He _____ a puzzle now. (has, had)

2. I _____ many races last year. (do, did)

3. They _____ a coin collection. (has, have)

4. Marco _____ dog grooming. (do, does)

5. Carly and I _____ the decorating now. (do, did)

6. Sara _____ an expensive painting. (has, have)

7. Henry and Lila _____ goats. (has, have)

8. We _____ go to bed early last night. (do, did)

9. Clive _____ fun at camp last summer. (has, had)

10. Angel _____ well at swim lessons. (do, does)

▶ **Revisit a piece of your writing. Edit the draft to make sure all irregular verbs are used correctly.**

Connect to Writing: Using Irregular Verbs

▶ **Read the selection and choose the best answer to each question.**

> *Axel wrote the following paragraph about crafts. Read his paragraph and look for any revisions he should make. Then answer the questions that follow.*

(1) We has a craft room in our house. (2) Mom and I do projects together. (3) We have lots of art supplies. (4) I want to make a collage with paper and paint. (5) Mom does the cutting. (6) I does the painting. (7) I would be happy if we did a craft every day!

1. In which sentences does the verb NOT match the subject?

A. Sentences 1 and 2

B. Sentences 2 and 3

C. Sentences 5 and 6

D. Sentences 1 and 6

2. What change, if any, should be made to sentence 6?

A. Change *I* to *We*.

B. Change *does* to *has*.

C. Change *does* to *do*.

D. Make no change.

▶ **Do you like making crafts? Write two or three sentences about a craft you enjoy.**

_____

_____

_____

_____

Grade 2 • Irregular Verbs

Action Verbs *Say, Eat, Run, Sit, Hide,* and *Tell*

The verbs *say, eat, run, sit, hide,* and *tell* are **irregular action verbs**. Do not add *-ed* to these verbs to tell about the past.

Present	Past
say, says	said
eat, eats	ate
run, runs	ran
sit, sits	sat
hide, hides	hid
tell, tells	told

▶ **Read each sentence and the word that tells when the action happens. Circle the word that correctly completes the sentence.**

1. The children (run, ran) to the swings. (present)

2. Parents (sit, sat) near the water fountain. (past)

3. Blake (hide, hid) behind a tree. (past)

4. Will and Pete (say, said) they are hungry. (present)

5. The families (ate, eat) a picnic lunch. (past)

▶ **Revisit a piece of your writing. Edit the draft to make sure irregular action verbs are used correctly.**

Action Verbs *Give, Take, See,* and *Go*

The verbs *give, take, see,* and *go* are **irregular action verbs**. Do not add *-ed* to these verbs to tell about the past.

Present	Past
give, gives	gave
take, takes	took
see, sees	saw
go, goes	went

▶ **Read each sentence and the word that tells when the action happens. Circle the word that correctly completes the sentence.**

1. They (go, went) with my mom to the store. (past)

2. We (take, took) the food into the house. (past)

3. Mom (gives, gave) Aunt Matilda a picture of me. (present)

4. Dad (see, saw) that dinner was ready. (past)

5. Then we all (go, went) into the living room to talk. (present)

▶ **Revisit a piece of your writing. Edit the draft to make sure irregular action verbs are used correctly.**

Using Action Verbs in the Present and Past

Irregular action verbs do not use *-ed* to form the past tense. The tables below show the present- and past-tense forms of common irregular verbs.

Present	Past
say, says	said
eat, eats	ate
run, runs	ran
sit, sits	sat
hide, hides	hid

Present	Past
tell, tells	told
give, gives	gave
take, takes	took
see, sees	saw
go, goes	went

▶ Read each sentence and the word that tells when the action happens. Then underline the correct verb that completes each sentence.

1. Sook (run, ran) to the bus stop. (past)

2. I (tell, told) Mr. Moreno the truth. (past)

3. Our friends (go, went) to the beach. (present)

4. We (take, took) a present to Ty. (present)

5. Feng (see, saw) the movie twice. (past)

▶ Revisit a piece of your writing. Edit the draft to make sure irregular action verbs are used correctly.

Review Irregular Action Verbs

The verbs *say, eat, run, sit, hide, tell, give, take, see,* and *go* are **irregular action verbs**. Do not add *-ed* to these verbs to tell what happened in the past.

▶ **Read the sentence and the word that tells when the action happens. Circle the word that correctly completes each sentence.**

1. We (run, ran) into the woods. (present)

2. Steve and Opal (eat, ate) apples. (present)

3. Alex and Ryan (say, said) we should play chase. (present)

4. We all (go, went) to different spots. (past)

5. Yaris and Tiana (hide, hid) in the bushes. (past)

6. Sam and Jay (sit, sat) quietly. (present)

7. Bill and Bryan (take, took) their backpacks. (past)

8. They (give, gave) each of us some nuts. (past)

9. We (tell, told) stories to each other. (present)

10. Val and Kam (see, saw) a bird. (past)

▶ **Revisit a piece of your writing. Edit the draft to make sure irregular action verbs are used correctly.**

Connect to Writing: Using Irregular Action Verbs

▶ **Read the selection and choose the best answer to each question.**

Penelope wrote the following story about an animal. Read her story and look for any revisions she should make. Then answer the questions that follow.

(1) A hamster was loose! (2) Whiskers escaped her cage. (3) Whiskers went down the hallway. (4) Ramone chased her. (5) He runned fast. (6) He finally caught Whiskers. (7) Ramone put Whiskers back in her cage.

1. Which of the following could replace sentence 3 to include an action verb?

A. Whiskers scampered down the hallway.

B. Whiskers went down the long hallway.

C. Whiskers was in the hallway.

D. Whiskers goes down the hallway.

2. What change, if any, should be made to sentence 5?

A. Change *runned* to *run*.

B. Change *runned* to *ran*.

C. Change *runned* to *ranned*.

D. Make no change.

▶ **What might happen if an animal escaped its cage or pen? Write two or three sentences about it.**

_____

_____

How Things Look, Feel, and Sound

> An **adjective** tells more about a noun. Adjectives can tell how a noun looks, feels, or sounds.

▶ **Write the adjective from the Word Bank that best fits each sentence. Use the clues in ( ).**

> green   hot   loud   soft   square

1. My dog Sammy has _____ fur. (feels)

2. That room has _____ walls. (looks)

3. We heard the _____ music. (sounds)

4. Tia carried a _____ package. (looks)

5. The _____ sun beat down on us. (feels)

▶ **Revisit a piece of your writing. Edit the draft to make sure adjectives that describe how things look, feel, and sound are used correctly.**

How Things Taste and Smell

An **adjective** tells more about a noun. Adjectives can tell how a noun tastes or smells.

▶ **In each sentence, find the adjective that tells more about the underlined noun. Write the adjective.**

1. I tried the salty <u>pretzels</u>. _____

2. We breathed the fresh <u>air</u>. _____

3. The strong <u>perfume</u> filled the room. _____

4. The sweet <u>berries</u> are ready to be picked. _____

5. I liked the sour <u>candy</u>. _____

▶ **Revisit a piece of your writing. Edit the draft to make sure adjectives that describe taste and smell are used correctly.**

Using Articles

A, an, and *the* are **articles**. Articles are special adjectives that point out certain nouns.

Use *a* and *an* with nouns that name only one. Use *a* with nouns that begin with a consonant sound. Use *an* with nouns that begin with a vowel sound.

The can be used with nouns that name one or more than one. *The* can be used with nouns that begin with a vowel sound or a consonant sound.

▶ **Write the correct article to complete each sentence.**

1. We saw _____ zebra at the zoo. (a, an)

2. Tracy plays _____ guitar. (an, the)

3. Her story won _____ prize. (a, an)

4. Did you hear _____ owl? (a, an)

5. I ate _____ apple. (a, the)

▶ **Revisit a piece of your writing. Edit the draft to make sure articles are used correctly.**

Review Adjectives and Articles

An **adjective** is a word that describes a noun. It can tell how something looks, tastes, smells, sounds, or feels.

Articles are special adjectives that point out certain nouns. The words *a*, *an*, and *the* are articles.

▶ **Circle the adjective in each sentence. Then write if the adjective describes how something looks, tastes, smells, sounds, or feels.**

1. I picked up the rough stone. _____

2. Casey wore silver boots. _____

3. I smelled the sweet flowers. _____

4. The noisy truck woke us up. _____

5. Sam spit out the bitter seeds. _____

6. Jane sat in the round chair. _____

▶ **Write the correct article to complete each sentence.**

7. Where is _____ house? (the, an)

8. Ellie has _____ new bike. (a, an)

9. Tim brought _____ cookies. (a, the)

10. Mia is _____ artist. (a, an)

▶ **Revisit a piece of your writing. Edit the draft to make sure articles and other adjectives are used correctly.**

Connect to Writing: Using Adjectives and Articles

▶ **Read the selection and choose the best answer to each question.**

> Trey wrote a passage about going berry picking. Read his paragraph and look for any revisions he should make. Then answer the questions that follow.

(1) We went to a farm. (2) We picked the red berries. (3) They made my fingers turn red! (4) Then we brought the berries home. (5) I helped make it pie. (6) The pie tasted good!

1. Which is the correct way to rewrite sentence 5?

A. I helped make a pie.

B. I helped make an pie.

C. I helped make a the pie.

D. I helped make an the pie.

2. Which adjective could tell you more about the pie in sentence 6?

A. pink

B. hard

C. sweet

D. loud

▶ **What is something you like to eat? Write two or three sentences about it. Use adjectives to add details and interest to your writing.**

_____

_____

_____

_____

Telling How Many

An **adjective** is a word that describes a noun. Numbers are special adjectives that tell **how many**.

Jane painted **one** cat.   Gary has **fifteen** dollars.

▶ **Draw a line under each adjective that tells how many. Write the noun it describes.**

1. Syd carried two bags. _____

2. Amy brought ten balloons. _____

3. Emme collected five leaves. _____

4. Anya swam twelve laps. _____

5. Ben bought six tickets. _____

▶ **Revisit a piece of your writing. Edit the draft to make sure adjectives that tell how many are used correctly.**

Adjectives with -er and -est

Add -er to adjectives to compare **two** people, animals, places, or things.

Add -est to compare **more than two** people, animals, places, or things.

Laura's house is **big**.

Bruce's house is **bigger** than Laura's.

Arial's house is the **biggest** of all three houses.

▶ **Write the correct adjective to complete each sentence.**

1. Jana is _____ than Mel. (faster, fastest)

2. The oak tree is _____ than the elm tree. (shorter, shortest)

3. Mark has the _____ voice in the choir. (lower, lowest)

4. Today is _____ than yesterday. (colder, coldest)

5. That is the _____ part of the pool. (deeper, deepest)

▶ **Revisit a piece of your writing. Edit the draft to make sure adjectives that compare are used correctly.**

Using Adjectives

Numbers are special adjectives that tell how many. When an adjective compares two things it ends in *-er*. When an adjective compares more than two things, it ends in *-est*.

▶ **Circle the adjective that tells how many.**

1. Our school has six grades.

2. Jason has two sisters.

3. The room had three closets.

4. Mel made eight cupcakes.

5. Simon found three golf balls.

▶ **Write the correct adjective to complete each sentence.**

6. The kitten is _____ than the puppy. (smaller, smallest)

7. It was the _____ movie I'd ever seen. (longer, longest)

8. Elle is _____ than Ann. (older, oldest)

9. Ice-skating is _____ than roller-skating. (harder, hardest)

10. I want to climb the _____ mountain in the United States. (steeper, steepest)

▶ **Revisit a piece of your writing. Edit the draft to make sure adjectives are used correctly.**

Review Using Adjectives

Numbers are special adjectives that tell how many. Adjectives can also be used to compare. Add *-er* to adjectives to compare nouns. Add *-est* to compare more than two.

Tells How Many	Compares Two	Compares More Than Two
Kate has **six** pencils.	Andre is **faster** than Rob.	Jon is the **fastest** boy in school.

▶ **Underline the adjective that tells how many.**

1. Will walked nine blocks.   2. Lisa wrote four poems.

3. The flight was six hours long.   4. Yara had eleven votes.

5. Three birds landed on the feeder.

▶ **Choose the correct adjective.**

6. Rose Street is _____ than Lily Street. (shorter, shortest)

7. This is the _____ room in the house. (larger, largest)

8. Skipper is _____ than Princess. (louder, loudest)

9. Steve is _____ than Dave. (younger, youngest)

10. We found the _____ place in the park. (quieter, quietest)

▶ **Revisit a piece of your writing. Edit the draft to make sure adjectives are used correctly.**

Connect to Writing: Using Adjectives

▶ **Read the selection and choose the best answer to each question.**

Cary wrote a passage about her brother Tom. Read her paragraph
and look for any revisions she should make. Then answer the questions
that follow.

(1) I have a brother named Tom. (2) He is younger than I am. (3) He is tallest
than me, but I am fastest. (4) We both like to read comics. (5) We make our own
comics, too. (6) He draws the pictures. (7) I write the words.

1. How can you improve sentence 2 by adding an adjective?

A. Tom is younger than I am.   **B.** He is my younger brother than I am.

C. Tom is younger years than I am.   **D.** He is two years younger than I am.

2. Which is the correct way to rewrite sentence 3?

A. He is tallest than me, but I am   **B.** He is taller than me, but I am
     faster.   fast.

C. He is taller than me, but I am faster.   **D.** He is tall than me, but I am fast.

▶ **Write about someone you know well. Tell how you are alike and how
you are different. Use adjectives that compare.**

_____

_____

_____

Adverbs That Tell How

> An **adverb** describes a verb. Adverbs can tell about how something is done.
>
> We lined up **quickly**.
> We got off the bus **slowly**.

▶ **Read each sentence. Think about the action. Then underline the adverb that tells how the action was done.**

1. Zina spoke quietly.

2. Raul sang loudly.

3. The principal spoke nicely to our guest.

4. We walked to school together.

5. The cat jumped softly off the table.

6. Jem clapped her hands excitedly.

7. Pete carefully stepped over the puddle.

8. Dave finished his homework quickly.

9. Gayle waited eagerly for the mail truck.

10. We all tried hard to win the game.

▶ **Revisit a piece of your writing. Edit the draft to make sure adverbs that tell how are used correctly.**

Adverbs That Tell When and Where

> An **adverb** describes a verb. Adverbs can tell about when or where an action happens.
>
> **First**, we bought our tickets.
> We waited **outside**.

▶ **Underline the adverb that tells when or where the action happened. Then write whether it tells when or where.**

1. The deer ran away. _____

2. Today we went to the park. _____

3. We will be home soon. _____

4. I bent down to see the ants. _____

5. We played inside. _____

▶ **Revisit a piece of your writing. Edit the draft to make sure adverbs that tell when and where are used correctly.**

Adjectives and Adverbs

An **adverb** describes a verb. Adverbs can tell how, when, or where an action happens. **Adjectives** describe nouns. Adjectives can tell how something looks, feels, sounds, tastes, or smells.

Adverb: The bunny hopped **quickly**.
Adjective: The **quick** bunny hopped away.

▶ **Underline the adverb or adjective that best completes each sentence.**

1. The driver parked the car (carefully, careful).

2. The (clever, cleverly) puppy opened the gate.

3. Tim walked (slowly, slow) to the door.

4. Peg whistled (cheerfully, cheerful) as we walked.

5. Soraya is a (smoothly, smooth) dancer.

6. Jed has a (loudly, loud) voice.

7. The choir sang (joyfully, joyful).

8. Una is a (strongly, strong) player.

9. The spotlight shines (bright, brightly).

10. The (shy, shyly) child stood behind his mom.

▶ **Revisit a piece of your writing. Edit the draft to make sure adjectives and adverbs are used correctly.**

Review Adverbs

An **adverb** is a word that describes a verb. An adverb can tell how an action happens. It can also tell when or where an action happens.

Tells How	Tells When	Tells Where
Jim worked **slowly**.	They will arrive **soon**.	The bird landed **nearby**.

▶ **Underline the adverb in each sentence. Then write whether it tells how, when, or where.**

1. The squirrel sat silently. _____

2. Then we visited Yan. _____

3. Yesterday we drove to Grandma's house. _____

4. We stood outside. _____

5. I ran swiftly across the playground. _____

6. Brad leaned over to pick a flower. _____

▶ **Underline the adverb or adjective that best completes each sentence.**

7. We laughed (loudly, loud).

8. The (weak, weakly) fence broke apart.

9. The (weird, weirdly) sound scared us.

10. Fred spoke (calm, calmly).

▶ **Revisit a piece of your writing. Edit the draft to make sure adverbs are used correctly.**

Grade 2 · Types of Adverbs

Connect to Writing: Using Adverbs

▶ **Read the selection and choose the best answer to each question.**

> *Sonya wrote a passage about riding a roller coaster. Read her paragraph and look for any revisions she should make. Then answer the questions that follow.*

(1) Yesterday we went to a theme park. (2) We rode the roller coaster. (3) We sat in a cart and put on seat belts. (4) Then the ride started with a jolt. (5) We raced up and down the hilly track. (6) I screamed loud. (7) It was scary, but I loved it!

1. Which adverb could you use after the word track to add the most interest to sentence 5?

A. soon

B. wildly

C. inside

D. after

2. Which is the correct way to write sentence 6?

A. I screamed loud!

B. I screamed louder!

C. I screamed loudest.

D. I screamed loudly.

▶ **Tell about something fun that you did recently. Write two or three sentences about it. Use adverbs to describe how, when, and where things happened.**

_____

_____

_____

Prepositions

A **preposition** is a word that tells where or when. It comes at the beginning of a prepositional phrase.

We swim **in the morning**. (when)
We swim **at the beach**. (where)

▶ **Write the preposition in each sentence on the line. Then underline the prepositional phrase.**

1. She napped after lunch. _____

2. They drove to the store. _____

3. We will have a picnic in the park. _____

4. He played ball at the park. _____

5. Luisa sat by her father. _____

▶ **Revisit a piece of your writing. Edit the draft to make sure prepositions are used correctly.**

Prepositional Phrases for Where

A **preposition** begins a prepositional phrase. A preposition can tell **where**.

A **prepositional phrase** is a group of words that can tell where something is.

in the attic   **by** the school   **on** the table

▶ **Write the prepositional phrase in each sentence on the line.**

1. Margot hurried down the hall. _____

2. The dog rolled in the grass. _____

3. Sunhil walked to the park. _____

▶ **Complete each sentence. Write a prepositional phrase that tells where.**

4. My cat climbs _____.

5. The duck swims _____.

▶ **Revisit a piece of your writing. Edit the draft to make sure prepositional phrases for where are used correctly.**

Prepositional Phrases for When

A **preposition** begins a prepositional phrase. A preposition can tell **when**.

A **prepositional phrase** is a group of words that can tell when something happens.

during the movie   **before** school   **after** the party

▶ **Circle the prepositional phrase in each sentence. Write the preposition on the line.**

1. We will meet at four o'clock. _____

2. The sun rises in the morning. _____

3. Meet me after class. _____

4. We stayed inside during the storm. _____

5. Wash your hands before you eat. _____

▶ **Revisit a piece of your writing. Edit the draft to make sure prepositional phrases for when are used correctly.**

Review Prepositions and Prepositional Phrases

A **preposition** is a word that joins with other words to tell **where** or **when**.

A **prepositional phrase** is a group of words that starts with a **preposition** and tells where something is or when something happens.

▶ **Underline the prepositional phrase in each sentence.**

1. We went hiking on the trail.

2. Hong rode his bike down the road.

3. The game begins at one o'clock.

4. Carlotta arrived before anyone else.

5. Grapes grow on a vine.

6. Acorns were on the ground.

▶ **For each sentence, add a prepositional phrase that tells where or when.**

7. The horse jumped _____.

8. Callie found her shoe _____.

9. We eat dinner _____.

10. My dad works _____.

▶ **Revisit a piece of your writing. Edit the draft to make sure prepositions and prepositional phrases are used correctly.**

Connect to Writing: Using Prepositions and Prepositional Phrases

▶ **Read the selection and choose the best answer to each question.**

Charles wrote a passage about a camping trip. Read his paragraph and look for any revisions he should make. Then answer the questions that follow.

(1) My family went camping. (2) We found a good site in the forest. (3) Mom and Dad set up the tent in the shade. (4) We went rafting down the river. (5) Then we fished before it got dark. (6) My parents cooked dinner over the fire. (7) We feel asleep after we told campfire tales.

1. Which two sentences have a prepositional phrase that tells where?

A. Sentences 1 and 2   **B.** Sentences 3 and 4

C. Sentences 4 and 5   **D.** Sentences 6 and 7

2. Which sentence has a prepositional phrase that tells when?

A. Sentence 1   **B.** Sentence 2

C. Sentence 4   **D.** Sentence 7

▶ **What outdoor activity have you done? Write two or three sentences about it. Use prepositional phrases that tell where or when.**

_____

_____

_____

Quotation Marks

> When you write, you show what someone says by putting **quotation marks (" ")** around the speaker's exact words.
>
> Julia said, "I am a painter."
> Miguel said, "I am a dancer."

▶ **Write each sentence. Put quotation marks around the speaker's exact words.**

1. Julia said, I always wanted to be a dancer.

_____

2. Miguel said, You can see us dance today.

_____

3. Ramon said, We will be dancing at the school.

_____

4. Julia asked, How can I learn to dance?

_____

5. Miguel answered, Come to class with me.

_____

▶ **Revisit a piece of your writing. Edit the draft to make sure quotation marks are used correctly.**

Commas in Quotations

Follow these rules when you use quotation marks.

1. Put a comma after words such as *said* and *asked*.

2. Begin the first word inside the quotation marks with a capital letter.

3. Put the end mark inside the quotation marks.

Kelsea said, "I walked to the park."

▶ **Draw a line under the sentence that is written correctly.**

1. Katie asked, "Are you going with us?"
   Katie asked "are you going with us?"

2. Kelsea said "I'm not sure I can go."
   Kelsea said, "I'm not sure I can go."

3. Katie asked, "Have you visited this park?"
   Katie asked, "Have you visited this park"

4. Kelsea said, "The park I visit is down the street."
   Kelsea said, "the park I visit is down the street."

5. Katie said, "OK, let's all go to that park today".
   Katie said, "OK, let's all go to that park today."

▶ **Revisit a piece of your writing. Edit the draft to make sure quotation marks are used correctly.**

Writing Quotations

> When you write, show what someone says by putting **quotation marks (" ")** at the beginning and end of the speaker's exact words.
>
> Brooke said, "I play softball."
> Rachel said, "I play volleyball."

▶ **Write each sentence. Put quotation marks around the speaker's exact words.**

1. Aimee asked, Will you play volleyball with us?

   _____

2. Rachel said, I will play on your team.

   _____

3. Brooke asked, Do you play softball, too?

   _____

4. Aimee answered, I like to play volleyball and softball.

   _____

5. Brooke said, Let's all play softball instead!

   _____

▶ **Revisit a piece of your writing. Edit the draft to make sure quotations are written correctly.**

Review Quotation Marks

Follow these rules when you use quotation marks.

1. Decide where to put the **comma**.

2. Begin the first word inside the quotation marks with a **capital letter**.

3. Put the **end mark** inside the quotation marks.

Becca asked, "Can you hear the wind?"

▶ **Draw a line under the correct sentence.**

1. Wanda said "I tap my foot to the beat."
   Wanda said, "I tap my foot to the beat."

2. Mr. Lorenz said, "It sounds great!"
   Mr. Lorenz said, "it sounds great!"

3. "I wrote the song" Becca said.
   "I wrote the song," Becca said.

4. Cari asked "Would you like to dance with us?"
   Cari asked, "Would you like to dance with us?"

5. Wanda said, "I love to dance."
   Wanda said "I love to dance."

▶ **Revisit a piece of your writing. Edit the draft to make sure quotation marks are used correctly.**

Connect to Writing: Using Quotation Marks

▶ **Read the selection and choose the best answer to each question.**

> *Shandra wrote the following paragraph about meeting her favorite artist. Read the paragraph and look for any revisions she should make. Then answer the questions that follow.*

(1) Yesterday I got to meet my favorite artist, Walter Smith. (2) I asked "How do you decide what to paint?" (3) Walter said, "I look for beautiful things during the day." (4) I asked, "What is one lovely thing you have painted?" (5) He said, "This morning, I painted my pretty pancake breakfast." (6) Finally, I asked him, "What is your favorite painting?" (7) He said I probably have not painted it yet. (8) It was so much fun to talk to him!

1. What correction, if any, needs to be made to sentence 2?

A. Add a comma after *I.*

B. Add a comma after *asked.*

C. Change *asked* to *said.*

D. Make no change.

2. Which of the following should replace sentence 7 to make it correct?

A. He said "I probably have not painted it yet."

B. "He said, I probably have not painted it yet."

C. He said "I probably have not painted it yet".

D. He said, "I probably have not painted it yet."

▶ **What is a conversation you had recently? Write two or three sentences about it. Make sure you use quotation marks correctly.**

_____

_____

Commas in Dates

A **date** tells the month, the number of the day, and the year.

Use a **comma (,)** between the **day** and the **year** in a date.

Evie was born **December 30, 2012**.

▶ **Write the date in each sentence. Put a comma in the correct place.**

1. He bought the horse on October 20 2015.

   _____

2. Mr. Santana sold his house on July 18 1998.

   _____

3. Alana's birthday party was June 4 2017.

   _____

4. The library opened on November 2 2011.

   _____

5. Ben got married on May 7 2005.

   _____

▶ **Revisit a piece of your writing. Edit the draft to make sure commas in dates are used correctly.**

Commas with Place Names

> Use a **comma (,)** between the name of a **city** or **town** and the
> name of a **state**.
>
> Miles flew to **Austin, Texas**.

▶ **Write the city and state named in each sentence. Put a comma
in the correct place.**

1. The sheep's wool comes from Columbus Ohio.

   _____

2. Missi moved to Portland Oregon.

   _____

3. Our next vacation will be in Honolulu Hawaii.

   _____

4. Linus has a meeting in Albany New York.

   _____

5. The Magnificent Mile is in Chicago Illinois.

   _____

▶ **Revisit a piece of your writing. Edit the draft to make sure
commas in place names are used correctly.**

Commas in Parts of a Letter

When you write a letter to someone, use a **comma (,)** after the **greeting** and the **closing** of the letter.

Dear Jerome,

How are you today? I am having fun here. Can you come over tomorrow?

Sincerely,

Tim

▶ **Write each letter greeting and closing. Put a comma in the correct place.**

1. Dear Maria _____

2. Sincerely _____

3. Best wishes _____

4. Dear Joaquin _____

5. Yours truly _____

▶ **Revisit a piece of your writing. Edit the draft to make sure commas are used correctly.**

Review Commas in Dates and Places

A **date** tells the month, the number of the day, and the year.
Use a **comma (,)** between the **day** and the **year** in a date.
For places, use a **comma (,)** between the name of a **city** or
town and the name of a **state**.
When you write a letter to someone, use a **comma (,)** after the
greeting and the **closing** of the letter.

▶ **Write the date or place in each sentence. Put a comma in the correct place.**

1. Ms. Ray moved to the farm on October 25 2016.

_____

2. Have you ever been to Savannah Georgia?

_____

3. She planted wheat on March 13 2017.

_____

4. We visited Houston Texas.

_____

5. Janie is from Asheville North Carolina.

_____

▶ **Revisit a piece of your writing. Edit the draft to make sure all commas in dates and places are used correctly.**

Connect to Writing: Using Commas in Dates and Places

▶ **Read the selection and choose the best answer to each question.**

> Anita wrote the following letter to her grandfather about her family's trip. Read the letter and look for any revisions she should make. Then answer the questions that follow.

(1) Dear Grandpa

(2) We went on a trip on June 17, 2018. (3) Our first stop was Galveston, Texas. (4) We stayed in a hotel on June 18, 2018. (5) Then we went to the Alamo Mission in San Antonio, Texas. (6) We came home on June 21 2018.

(7) Sincerely,

(8) Anita

1. Which of the following should replace sentence 1 to make it correct?

A. Dear Grandpa.

B. Dear Grandpa,

C. Dear, Grandpa

D. Dear Grandpa;

2. Which of the following should replace sentence 6 to make it correct?

A. We came home on, June 21 2018.

B. We came home on June, 21 2018.

C. We came home on June 21, 2018.

D. We came home on June, 21, 2018.

▶ **What is a place you have visited recently? What date did you visit? Write two or three sentences about it. Be sure to use commas correctly for dates and places.**

Commas in a Series of Nouns

You can list nouns in a series. A **series of nouns** is three or more nouns that appear together in a sentence.

When you list three or more nouns, use a comma after each noun in the series except for the last noun.

My brother plays **baseball, football, and hockey**.

Our school also has teams for **volleyball, basketball, and track**.

▶ **Draw a line under each correct sentence.**

1. Kevin, Philip, and Carlos like to play baseball.

   Kevin, Philip and Carlos, like to play baseball.

2. There are books, pictures and candles on the shelf.

   There are books, pictures, and candles on the shelf.

3. The doctor treats dogs, cats and rabbits.

   The doctor treats dogs, cats, and rabbits.

4. We see children, parents, and pets at the park.

   We see children, parents and, pets at the park.

5. Blair put oranges grapes, and pineapple in her cart.

   Blair put oranges, grapes, and pineapple in her cart.

▶ **Revisit a piece of your writing. Edit the draft to make sure commas in a series are used correctly.**

Commas in a Series of Verbs

You can list verbs in a series. A **series of verbs** is three or more verbs that appear together in a sentence.

When you list three or more verbs, use a comma after each verb in a series except the last verb.

The team **runs, shoots, and scores**.

▶ **Look at the underlined series of verbs in each sentence. Write each sentence correctly. Put commas in the correct places.**

1. The batter swings hits and runs.

   _____

2. The pitcher pauses looks and throws the ball.

   _____

3. The fans clap cheer and yell.

   _____

4. The coach points signals and nods.

   _____

5. The mascot dances jumps and rolls.

   _____

▶ **Revisit a piece of your writing. Edit the draft to make sure commas in a series are used correctly.**

Writing Series of Nouns and Verbs

> You can list nouns or verbs in a series. A **series of nouns or verbs** is three or more nouns or verbs that appear together in a sentence. Use a comma after each noun or verb in a series except the last one.
>
> I heard **owls, crickets, and frogs**.   The turtle **crawls, stops, and rests**.

▶ **Write words from the word box to complete each sentence. Use commas and the word** *and.*

| sneakers | boots | slippers |

1. Harlan has _____

| sing | dance | act |

2. Stephen can _____

| pasta | bread | salad |

3. Frances ate _____

| toothbrush | pillow | pajamas |

4. Jamal brought his _____

| jumps | dives | swims |

5. Frances _____

▶ **Revisit a piece of your writing. Edit the draft to make sure commas in a series are used correctly.**

Review Commas in a Series

When you list a series of three or more nouns or verbs, use a comma after each noun or verb except the last one.

I ate **berries, cake, and jam**.   She **tripped, stumbled, and fell**.

▶ **Rewrite each sentence and add commas where they belong.**

1. The farm has dogs hens and goats.

    _____

2. The bull kicks jumps and runs.

    _____

3. We fed the pigs chickens and cows.

    _____

4. I played with the kittens puppies and chicks.

    _____

5. The farmer plows plants and rakes.

    _____

▶ **Revisit a piece of your writing. Edit the draft to make sure commas in a series are used correctly.**

Connect to Writing: Using Commas in a Series

▶ **Read the selection and choose the best answer to each question.**

> *Chen wrote the following paragraph about going to the beach. Read the paragraph and look for any revisions he should make. Then answer the questions that follow.*

(1) I just went to the beach with my friend Tessa. (2) We swam played and explored. (3) We saw seagulls, hermit crabs, and fish. (4) We had breakfast, lunch, and, dinner, by the sea. (5) We also sat, relaxed, and talked. (6) We packed up and drove home. (7) I hope we go back again soon!

1. Which sentence, if any, should replace sentence 2 to make it correct?

A. We swam, played, and explored.   **B.** We swam played, and explored.

C. We swam, played, and, explored.   **D.** Make no change.

2. Which sentence, if any, should replace sentence 4 to make it correct?

A. We had breakfast, lunch, and, dinner by the sea.

B. We had breakfast lunch, and dinner by the sea.

C. We had breakfast, lunch, and dinner by the sea.

D. We had breakfast, lunch and dinner, by the sea.

▶ **What are three things you have seen or done recently? Write two or three sentences about it. Remember to use commas in a series.**

_____

_____

_____

Contractions with *Not*

A **contraction** is a short way of writing two words. An **apostrophe (')**
shows where letters were left out.

Whole Words		Contraction	
do not	is not	don't	isn't
does not	cannot	doesn't	can't

▶ **Write a contraction for the underlined word or words in each sentence.**

1. Kiki <u>does not</u> have her doll. _____

2. She <u>is not</u> sure where to go. _____

3. Her friends <u>are not</u> home. _____

4. Kiki <u>cannot</u> find her shoes. _____

5. They <u>were not</u> under the bed. _____

6. The shoes <u>do not</u> have laces. _____

7. They <u>are not</u> in the closet. _____

8. The doll <u>is not</u> with them, either. _____

9. Kiki <u>did not</u> tell her mom. _____

10. Her brother <u>cannot</u> help. _____

▶ **Revisit a piece of your writing. Edit the draft to make sure contractions
are used correctly.**

Contractions with Pronouns

A **contraction** is a word made by putting two words together.

An **apostrophe** replaces the letter or letters that are left out.

Many contractions are made by joining a **pronoun** and a **verb**.

Two Words	Contraction
I am	I'm
You will She will	You'll She'll
We are They are	We're They're
She is It is	She's It's

▶ **Write a contraction for the underlined words in each sentence.**

1. We are going to our house. _____

2. They are going, too. _____

3. You are invited to come. _____

4. Hector says he is hungry. _____

5. Jill says she is thirsty. _____

6. Lyle says it is hot outside. _____

7. Gail says she will ride bikes. _____

8. Shim says he will go with her. _____

9. I think it is my turn to wash dishes. _____

10. You will enjoy the play. _____

▶ **Revisit a piece of your writing. Edit the draft to make sure contractions are used correctly.**

Forming Contractions

A **contraction** is a short way of writing two words. An **apostrophe (')** shows where letters were left out. Many contractions are made with the word *not*. Many contractions are also made by joining a **pronoun** and a **verb**.

Two Words		Contraction	
She is	They are	She's	They're
I am	Do not	I'm	Don't

▶ **Write a contraction for the underlined words in each sentence.**

1. We are playing in the sandbox. _____

2. Cara said she is digging. _____

3. He is filling the holes with water. _____

4. Gus and Emma said they are building. _____

5. This day could not get any better! _____

▶ **Revisit a piece of your writing. Edit the draft to make sure contractions are used correctly.**

Review Contractions

A **contraction** is a word made by putting two words together. An **apostrophe** replaces the letter or letters that are left out. Many contractions are made with the word **not**. Many contractions are also made by joining a **pronoun** and a **verb**.

▶ **Write a contraction for the underlined word or words in each sentence.**

1. Put things away so they <u>do not</u> get lost. _____

2. The banjo <u>is not</u> where it should be. _____

3. Angela <u>cannot</u> find the muffin tin. _____

4. She <u>does not</u> know where to look. _____

5. <u>We are</u> going to help her find it. _____

6. Jon and Susie said <u>they are</u> helping, too. _____

7. <u>You will</u> see that we will find it. _____

8. <u>I am</u> sure it will be found. _____

9. Then <u>we will</u> enjoy some muffins. _____

10. <u>They are</u> not ready yet! _____

▶ **Revisit a piece of your writing. Edit the draft to make sure contractions are used correctly.**

Connect to Writing: Using Contractions

▶ **Read the selection and choose the best answer to each question.**

> *Penny wrote the following paragraph about knitting. Read her story and look for any revisions she should make. Then answer the questions that follow.*

(1) My hobby is knitting. (2) I'm very good at it. (3) There arn't a lot of people who knit. (4) My friends think it's neat! (5) Sometimes theyl watch me knit. (6) I've made hats and scarves for my friends. (7) They come in all colors. (8) Knitting is a great hobby.

1. What is the correct spelling of the contraction *arn't* in sentence 3?

A. ar'ent

B. are'not

C. aren't

D. arn't

2. What change, if any, should be made to sentence 5?

A. Change *theyl* to *theyll*.

B. Change *theyl* to *they'll*.

C. Change *theyl* to *they'ill*.

D. Make no change.

▶ **What do you like to do for a hobby? Write two or three sentences about it. Include some contractions.**

_____

_____

_____

Abbreviations for Titles for People

A title may be used before a person's name.

A title begins with a capital letter and usually ends with a period.

Mrs. LaSalle is a baker.   **Dr.** Jenkins works with children.

▶ **Write each underlined title and name correctly.**

1. My friend <u>mr Woods</u> saw me at the park. _____

2. I saw <u>mrs Gupta</u> there, too. _____

3. We all bought ice cream from <u>miss Miller</u>. _____

4. We waved to <u>dr Mak</u>. _____

5. His nurse is <u>ms Adams</u>. _____

6. One lady, <u>mrs Garcia</u>, watched children play. _____

7. Her husband is <u>mr Garcia</u>. _____

8. They took their dog to see <u>dr Taneja</u>. _____

9. Was that <u>ms Thomas</u> on a bike? _____

10. I think it was <u>miss Bodo</u>. _____

▶ **Revisit a piece of your writing. Edit the draft to make sure abbreviations for people's titles are written correctly.**

Abbreviations for Days and Months

Each day of the week can be written in a short way, called an **abbreviation**.

Mon. Tues. Wed. Thurs. Fri. Sat. Sun.

Some months of the year can also be written in a short way. Notice that May, June, and July do not have a shortened form.

Jan.	Apr.	July	Oct.
Feb.	May	Aug.	Nov.
Mar.	June	Sept.	Dec.

▶ **Write the abbreviation for each underlined word.**

1. Miss Elliot went fishing on <u>Saturday</u>. _____

2. We will have a picnic on <u>Sunday</u>. _____

3. My favorite month is <u>December</u>. _____

4. I write in my journal every <u>Wednesday</u>. _____

5. My birthday is in <u>March</u>. _____

6. The leaves change colors in <u>September</u>. _____

7. We will visit Grandma in <u>April</u>. _____

8. The movie comes out on <u>Thursday</u>. _____

9. We got our dog in <u>February</u>. _____

10. We pick vegetables in <u>August</u>. _____

▶ **Revisit a piece of your writing. Edit the draft to make sure abbreviations for days and months are written correctly.**

Abbreviations for Places

An **abbreviation** is a shortened form of a longer word. The names of places are proper nouns that can be shortened. Abbreviations for proper nouns begin with a capital letter.

▶ **Write the abbreviation for each underlined word.**

1. I live on Elm Street. _____

2. My friend lives on Gloria Drive. _____

3. Mr. Peabody owns a shop on Main Street. _____

4. Our school is on Lincoln Avenue. _____

5. We play kickball on Tracie Court. _____

6. Mrs. Dean is looking at a house on Mason Drive. _____

7. The best pizza place is on Wilkins Road. _____

8. There is a party at 458 Westside Circle. _____

9. Cars move along Spring Avenue. _____

10. Carson Road is a busy street. _____

▶ **Revisit a piece of your writing. Edit the draft to make sure abbreviations for places are written correctly.**

Review Abbreviations

> The names of days, months, and places are proper nouns that can be shortened. An **abbreviation** is a short way to write a word by taking out some of the letters and writing a period at the end. Abbreviations for proper nouns begin with a capital letter.

▶ **Write the correct abbreviation for each underlined word.**

1. Our babysitter, <u>mrs</u> Ortiz, took a message. _____

2. The couch would be delivered on <u>Tuesday</u>. _____

3. The delivery man is <u>mr</u> Robson. _____

4. It was due in <u>October</u>. _____

5. But the van came in <u>November</u>. _____

6. The couch came on a <u>Friday</u>. _____

7. They went to 881 <u>Blazing Street</u>. _____

8. But, it was supposed to go to <u>Blake Road</u>. _____

9. Now, <u>dr</u> Lane has a new couch! _____

10. A table will come in <u>April</u>. _____

▶ **Revisit a piece of your writing. Edit the draft to make sure abbreviations are written correctly.**

Connect to Writing: Using Abbreviations

▶ **Read the selection and choose the best answer to each question.**

> *Fiona wrote the following paragraph about a family trip. Read her story and look for any revisions she should make. Then answer the questions that follow.*

(1) My family and I went on a trip. (2) We took our neighbor, mrs. Fields, with us. (3) Our trip was planned in June. (4) But the weather was bad, so we left in July. (5) We met Mr. Rogers on Sat. (6) He runs the shell shop on George St. (7) We visited many other neat places. (8) We met lots of fun people.

1. What is the correct way to write the abbreviation mrs. in sentence 2?

A. Mrss

B. Mis.

C. Mrs.

D. Mrs

2. What change, if any, should be made to sentence 4?

A. Change *July* to *Ju*.

B. Change *July* to *Jul*.

C. Change *July* to *Ju'ly*.

D. Make no change.

▶ **Where do you like to go with your family? Write two or three sentences about it. Use some abbreviations.**

_____

_____

_____

Spelling: Words with Vowel Teams

Vowel Team	Sound	Examples
ai, ay	long a	bait, ray
ee, ea	long e	feet, bead
oa, ow	long o	coat, blow
ew, oo, ou	$\overline{oo}$	new, root, soup
oo	$\breve{oo}$	foot, cook

▶ **Write the correct spelling of each underlined word.**

1. Jani and Irwin will swim in the pule. _____

2. Gavin lade his towel on the chair. _____

3. Sandy can reech the deep end. _____

4. Ryu will shoe everyone how to dive. _____

5. There is a toy bote in the water. _____

6. Hannah swims with great spede. _____

7. Mae wates in line for the slide. _____

8. Mr. Ingalls cokes hotdogs on the grill. _____

9. Kara bleu bubbles in the water. _____

10. Everyone's teath chatter from the cold. _____

▶ **Revisit a piece of your writing. Edit the draft to make sure all words are spelled correctly.**

Spelling Words with Endings

If a word ends in a consonant, double the consonant and add -ed or -ing. If a word ends in an -e, drop the -e and add -ed or -ing. Some endings change a word's meaning: -less means "without"; -ful means "full of"; -ly tells how.

Add the Ending	Miss Jacobs was **helping** Victor.
Double the Consonant	Victor was **sitting** still.
Drop the -e	Victor was no longer **confused**.
Use -less, -ful, or -ly	Miss Jacobs was **helpful**.

▶ **Write the correct spelling of each underlined word.**

1. Emma took a cookie when no one was watcheing. _____

2. Geraldo saw her eatting the cookie. _____

3. Their dog waged its tail. _____

4. Emma shareed some cookie with the dog. _____

5. The dog chewed it slowley. _____

6. Geraldo asket if he could have some, too. _____

7. Emma was selflese and gave him one. _____

8. Geraldo smileed and said, "Thank you." _____

9. Geraldo was carefull not to drop any crumbs. _____

10. The three enjoyyed their mid-day snack together. _____

Spelling: High-Frequency Words

Some words that are used a lot in writing do not follow a spelling pattern. It is important to learn to spell them correctly.

Common Words

been, buy, call, first, goes, many, which, people

▶ **Write the correct spelling of each underlined word.**

1. Mrs. Evans <u>gaev</u> Tamika money for the movies. _____

2. Tamika invited her <u>bessed</u> friend, Kim. _____

3. They are <u>bothe</u> excited about the movie! _____

4. There are <u>meny</u> people at the movie. _____

5. They watched ads <u>bifore</u> the movie started. _____

6. Someone said the movie <u>wod</u> start soon. _____

7. Tamika was a little <u>coled</u>. _____

8. She put a jacket <u>arownd</u> her legs. _____

9. The movie was <u>vary</u> good. _____

10. Tamika and Kim <u>sed</u> they would see it again! _____

▶ **Revisit a piece of your writing. Edit the draft to make sure all words are spelled correctly.**

Review Spelling

To help you spell correctly, remember vowel teams.

Words with Vowel Teams: plain, cream, boat, crow, flew

Some words don't have vowel teams, so you have to learn to spell them.

High-Frequency Words: many, should, because

▶ **Write the correct spelling of each underlined word.**

1. The treehouse was made of <u>would</u>. _____

2. Anu decided to <u>clene</u> it up a bit. _____

3. Levi tried to <u>clame</u> it as his own. _____

4. Anu said she would share it if he helped her <u>paynt</u>. _____

5. Levi <u>jumpt</u> right in! _____

6. He was being very <u>carful</u>. _____

7. The two <u>maid</u> the best treehouse ever! _____

8. Before long, they were <u>siting</u> in the treehouse. _____

9. They invited other <u>peeple</u> to come. _____

10. But Anu and Levi were the <u>furst</u> to enjoy it. _____

▶ **Revisit a piece of your writing. Edit the draft to make sure all words are spelled correctly.**

Connect to Writing: Using Correct Spelling

▶ **Read the selection and choose the best answer to each question.**

> *Ari wrote the following paragraph about skateboarding. Read his story and look for any revisions he should make. Then answer the questions that follow.*

(1) I like skateboarding with my friends. (2) We often go skateing at the skate park. (3) Raj does flips and turns. (4) Cybil could ride for hours! (5) Brandon does simple tricks. (6) We all chear each other on. (7) We look forward to another day of skateboarding.

1. What is the correct way to spell the word *skateing* in sentence 2?

A. skating   **B.** skaeting

C. skatting   **D.** skateeing

2. What change, if any, should be made to sentence 6?

A. Change *all* to *awl*.   **B.** Change *chear* to *cheer*.

C. Change *other* to *othar*.   **D.** Make no change.

▶ **What do you like to do with your friends? Write two or three sentences about it.**

_____

_____

_____

_____